C000104501

M 25

M25

Summersdale Publishers Ltd
46 West Street
Chichester
West Sussex
PO19 1RP
UK

www.summersdale.com

Printed and bound in the Czech Republic

ISBN: 978-1-84953-769-8

Substantial discounts on bulk quantities of Summersdale books are available to corporations, professional associations and other organisations. For details contact Nicky Douglas by telephone: +44 (0) 1243 756902, fax: +44 (0) 1243 786300 or email: nicky@summersdale.com.

A Circular Tour of the London Orbital

RAY HAMILTON

summersdale

For Karen, in the year
of our very own M25!

Acknowledgements

My thanks to all at Summersdale Publishers, and to Claire Plimmer and Debbie Chapman in particular, for the opportunity and support to write another book on another very different subject. My thanks also to Julian Beecroft for his thorough final edit.

Contents

⟦⟧ Introduction

The M25 is a form of social control to ensure disruptive elements in society are neutralised by keeping a significant proportion of them in continual motion.

Will Self

There has never been a more talked-about road in Britain than the M25 motorway round London. Its regular traffic reports are as British as the latest weather news and the shipping forecast. Every day it plays transient host to a seething mass of humanity on the move, a mass that includes commuters, supermarket delivery drivers, British and foreign truckers, jacket-on-a-hanger salesmen, tradesmen, day trippers, tourists, visiting relatives, football teams and their fans, airport-goers, Channel Tunnel-goers, festival-goers and many other goers besides.

When the M25 works, it works, slashing journey times round London and on to destinations in Britain and beyond. When it doesn't work, the knives come out. Highways England (formerly the Highways Agency) is vilified alongside politicians, urban planners, road construction companies, bad drivers, the emergency services and anyone else who might possibly be responsible for delaying motorists' lives for a matter of minutes or occasionally hours.

The road took 11 years to build between 1975 and 1986, but the need for an orbital route round London was being talked about as early as 1905, when the city streets were already congested with horse-drawn traffic, early motor cars and the first electric tramcars. But for every visionary and urban planner, there would in time be a hundred conscientious objectors, those who had cast-iron reasons why their plot of land should not under any circumstances be interfered with, or why their eyes and ears should not be offended by the sights and sounds of a monstrous motorway designed for the benefit of others. It was never going to be easy, then, and perhaps it was more than symbolic that it was driven through to completion during the Thatcher years, for this was a prime minister who had long experience of dealing with meddlesome people intent on interfering with her ideals. If she could handle the miners, the trade unionists and General Galtieri, she could probably handle a few thousand road objectors.

But the objectors in fact won many battles, before and after Thatcher took office. The changes they brought about saved whole communities from the invading army of diggers, but they also resulted in a motorway that cost more, took longer to build, couldn't cope with demand, and often had to be built through terrain that was far from ideal from a construction point of view. Embankments were built high, chalk was dug deep so that hills might be scaled rather than skirted, interchanges were complicated and enough trees were planted to create a circular forest. Engineering triumph after engineering triumph protected many of the towns and villages of outer London from the motorway and conversely denied the motorway's users many fine views of the Home Counties.

There are still many sights to be enjoyed while 'driving the doughnut', however, and many more still by exiting the motorway at any of its 33 junctions to seek out the often hidden treasures beyond. This book tries to look beyond the obvious and seeks to enlighten and enhance our enjoyment of a 117-mile (188-km) circular road to nowhere that ultimately, one way or another, leads to everywhere.

History in the Making

1905

At a time when horse-drawn transport still existed
alongside early motor cars and electric tramways, a
Royal Commission loosely proposed a circular road
round London to ease congestion, the route of which
was quite similar to what we know today as the North
and South Circular roads. Water troughs would have
served as 'service stations', and wheelwrights and
farriers would have been needed to provide breakdown
services, acting as the AA of their day.

1920s

A rudimentary version of what is now known as
the North Circular (or A406) was built as part of

an unemployment relief scheme following the First World War.

1926

Italy under Mussolini became the first country in the world to build a fast road reserved for motor vehicles, an autostrada that ran from Milan to the Italian lakes.

1935

Germany's first autobahn was completed between Frankfurt and Darmstadt.

1935

A somewhat tortuous chain of streets round south London were deemed sufficiently well connected to be dubbed the South Circular Road (or A205). I suspect that much smoke and many mirrors were present in the Ministry of Transport the day that decision was taken.

1937

The Highways Development Survey drawn up by engineer Sir Charles Bressey and his consultant Sir Edwin Lutyens provided the first coherent proposal for an orbital road round Greater London, at a radial distance of 18 to 20 miles (29 to 32 km) from Charing Cross. The Second World War put paid to their grand plans, but the route they devised for the South Orbital section in particular is pretty much followed by the M25 today.

1944

As part of the blueprint for post-war reconstruction, and taking advantage of the opportunities that bomb-damaged areas presented on a scale not seen since the Great Fire of London in 1666, architect and town planner Sir Patrick Abercrombie drew up the Greater London Plan, including five ring roads. To some extent this was an update of the Bressey/Lutyens pre-war plan, but the outer ring now stretched as far as 30 miles (48 km) out from Charing Cross. The optimism of the plan was most welcome in the post-war circumstances then prevailing, but the depressed economic climate didn't allow for it to get off the ground. Abercrombie still went down in road history, though, as the first man to use the word 'motorway'.

1950s

Britain's roads became like clogged arteries in need of open-heart surgery as more and more slow-moving vehicles belched out fumes and leaked petrol and oil around its towns and countryside. Motorists grew impatient for the promised motorways that would offer speed and freedom to all.

1958

Britain's first stretch of motorway, the 8-mile-long (13-km-long) Preston bypass that would later be subsumed within the M6, was opened by Prime Minister

Harold Macmillan, thereby relieving congestion on the main artery between England and Scotland.

1959

Transport Minister Ernest Marples opened the M1, Britain's first complete motorway, which ran from St Albans in Hertfordshire to Dunchurch in Warwickshire. At the opening ceremony Marples warned motorists that 'travelling at speeds hitherto unknown, senses may be numbed and judgement warped'.

1960s

Road safety became a major concern in Britain because of the appalling standard of driving on its motorways. Without speed limits or seat belts, and with no crash barriers between carriageways, head-on collisions at high speed became all too common.

Safety Last

Apparently, motorists were so naive in the 1960s that they needed public information films and a regularly updated Highway Code to explain the very basics to them. Until these were produced, motorists who missed their motorway exits would reverse or even do a three-point turn to get back on track. It didn't seem to occur to them either that flooring the pedal for mile after mile in a clapped-out, poorly maintained car might cause the car to overheat and die of exhaustion – the main reason for the AA or RAC being called to a motorway breakdown was to deliver the last rites to a big end.

Motorists were accordingly outraged when in 1966 Transport Minister Barbara Castle announced a preliminary 70-mph (113-km/h) speed limit, but by 1969 speed limits, seat belts and breathalysers had become law.

1961

The Ministry of Transport set up the London Traffic Survey to establish a comprehensive picture of transport in and around London and to forecast how this would change in future.

Nice Work If You Can Get It

It took a glut of British and American consultants three years to provide the comprehensive picture needed for the London

Traffic Survey, and a further two years to develop forecasting procedures and estimates of future traffic levels. Their findings were so alarming that they convinced the Ministry of Transport that more sophisticated analytical techniques would be required over a number of extra years to conclude the detailed evaluation required and possibly, just possibly, make some recommendations for the future. I'm fairly sure none of the consultants struggled to pay their mortgages by the time they were finished.

1967

Building on the London Traffic Survey, a proposed London Ringway Scheme planned to upgrade the North and South Circulars to motorway standard and to have them form one of four concentric roads round the capital. This innermost ring was to be known as Ringway 1, or the London Motorway Box, and would involve the destruction of tens of thousands of houses and the displacement of hundreds of thousands of residents across every inner borough of the capital. The government had apparently lost the plot and public protests were loud and strong, but the scheme was still incorporated into the 1969 Greater London

Development Plan. The planned madness was finally cancelled in 1973 after the GLC (Greater London Council) bowed to pressure applied by the Homes Before Roads political movement.

1970s ONWARDS

As traffic levels mushroomed around London, Capital Radio did its level best to keep motorists with revolutionary in-car radio informed about incidents and delays, including reports provided from the mid seventies onwards from the Flying Eye, a twin-engine light aircraft kitted out for the purpose. Their reporter in the sky for 20 years (between 1984 and 2004) was writer and broadcaster Russ Kane, who clocked up 10,000 flying hours and 1.5 million air miles without ever having his seat upgraded. He achieved more circuits of the M25 than any other man alive, but without any of the delays.

Conscientious Objectors

After decades of listening to motorists bleating about congestion, successive British governments presided over the building of longed-for motorways, including the M25 from 1975 onwards, only to discover that the mood of the public had changed in favour of protecting the environment at local, national and planetary levels. The modernism that had been worshipped by the masses for 40 years was suddenly seen as the enemy of the people and their endangered surroundings.

The public's imagination was well and truly captured in 1973 when the Upshire Preservation Society mounted a campaign to prevent the planned M16 (which was to become part of the M25) ploughing through the pretty village of Upshire in the Epping Forest. The protestors parked their tractors, combine harvesters and horseboxes in Parliament Square before marching slowly along Whitehall with Vanessa the goat leading the way ahead of memorable banners that read 'Not Epping Likely!'

The tide of public opinion had turned and for the next decade you couldn't find a government minister to turn up and open a stretch of motorway. In that very British way of lampooning politics gone mad, the arts soon entered the fray. Tom Sharpe's hilarious 1975 book and the accompanying TV series, *Blott on the Landscape*, centred around an anti-motorway protest which caricatured the ongoing battle between the landed gentry and an unholy alliance of interfering politicians and invasive road-builders. Douglas Adams' *Hitchhikers Guide to the Galaxy*, which started in 1978 as a radio comedy, went further into the realms of the ridiculous with the planned destruction of planet earth to make way for an interspace highway. The BBC took things more seriously in 1982 with *Boys from the Black Stuff*, a humorous but nonetheless poignant drama series about the impact of the Thatcher era on a gang of Liverpudlian tarmac layers struggling to make ends meet.

The Public Enquiries of the M25

By the mid seventies the government was becoming increasingly fearful of the protest lobby so they tried the salami approach with the M25, slicing up the route and therefore the public consultation process into 39 separate public enquiries to deal with all the objections raised. Divide and rule was the order of the day.

The length of the enquiries varied from a single day to one that dragged on for 97 sitting days over a 13-month period, and many of the statutory proposals had to go before Parliament. For example, Epping Forest remains protected as a public space under the Epping Forest Act of 1878 and was further declared a Site of Special Scientific Interest in 1953, so you can't just steamroller your way through it without parliamentary assent.

As an example of the procedures involved to get approval for one salami slice, in 1974 the 13-mile (21-km) length between J14 (Heathrow) and J17 (Rickmansworth) went to public consultation with five optional routes. Some 15,000 questionnaires were distributed and over 5,000 were completed and returned. The preferred route was announced in 1976 and the proposals were advertised formally under Highways Act procedures in 1978. These attracted some 2,000 objections and a public inquiry was held between October 1979 and May 1980, during which time objectors put forward several alternative routes. The Department of Transport had to provide economic and environmental comparisons between their own proposed route and each and every proposed alternative route. The Inspector did finally find in the Department's favour, at least as far as the basic route was concerned, and the Secretary of State for Transport accepted the decision in 1982. Construction could finally get underway on that stretch of the motorway.

No public enquiry stopped a single stretch of motorway being built, but collectively the objections changed the way the M25 and every other motorway would be built in Britain henceforth, as the inspectors required plan after plan to be amended to protect residential areas, the countryside, flora, fauna, birdlife, insect life and everything else that had not been valued previously by successive modernising governments. Diversions, deep cuttings, noise-reducing mounds of earth, soundproof fences and cosmetic screens composed of millions of trees and shrubs and hedges were just some of the time-consuming and costly measures that would have to be factored into road-building business cases for evermore. Feelings had run high throughout the consultation process, with Department of Transport officials being threatened and pursued to their homes at the end of a day's proceedings, and the government was once more left in little doubt about the strength of public outrage when it came to building roads without due care and attention to the environment and the lives of the people who elected them in the first place.

The Number of Lanes Required

Many M25 objectors in the seventies argued that the motorway needed to be just two lanes wide on each carriageway, claiming in the aftermath of the 1973 oil crisis that the Department of Transport's forecast traffic figures were too high because oil shortages would inevitably lead to less traffic. The DoT's forecasts were in fact woefully low, and deliberately so. Having paid huge sums of money to consultants to have it confirmed, they must have known that four-lane carriageways would be the minimum requirement from the start, but they also knew that the road might never get built if they pushed their luck too far too soon, so they went for three-lane carriageways as a compromise and left it to future generations of DoT officials to widen the motorway as best they could.

1975

The Department of Transport announced that the planned orbital roads to the north (M16) and south (M25) of the capital would be subsumed into a single ring road – the London Orbital Motorway – which would be known in shorthand from that point on as the M25. Later that same year Balfour Beatty completed the first section of the newly designated M25, between J23 (South Mimms) and J24 (Potters Bar). The London Orbital was up and running.

1982

Sir Horace Cutler, leader of the Greater London Council (GLC) from 1977 to 1981, pushed hard for the M25 to be built. When the route between J16 (M40) and J17 (Maple Cross) was announced in 1982, he was perhaps surprised to learn that it was to cut through the grounds of his family home in Gerrards Cross, Buckinghamshire.

Piece by Piece

The M25 appears nowadays as a single entity but was developed in piecemeal fashion. As we have seen, different stretches had to be proposed, justified, objected to, planned, developed and built in their own right. The louder the objections, the longer the statutory process. The longer the statutory process, the later that particular stretch of road was built and opened to the travelling public. Here is the timeline of what must have looked like very random progress towards the completion of the whole:

Month/year	Junctions	Area covered
September 1975	J23–J24	Bignell's Corner (South Mimms) to Potters Bar
February 1976	J6–J8	Godstone to Reigate
February 1976	J17–J19	Maple Cross to Chandler's Cross
December 1976	J12–J13	Thorpe (M3) to Runnymede
April 1977	J1–J3	Dartford to Swanley (M20)
November 1979	J5–J6	Chevening to Godstone
October 1980	J11–J12	Addlestone to Thorpe (M3)
June 1981	J24–J25	Potters Bar to Waltham Cross
August 1982	J13–J14	Runnymede to Poyle (Heathrow Airport)
December 1982	J29–J31	Cranham to Purfleet

April 1983	J27–J29	Theydon Bois (M11) to Cranham
December 1983	J10–J11	Wisley to Addlestone
January 1984	J25–J27	Waltham Cross to Theydon Bois (M11)
January 1985	J16–J17	Denham (M40) to Maple Cross
September 1985	J15–J16	Colnbrook (M4) to Denham (M40)
October 1985	J8–J10	Reigate to Wisley
December 1985	J14–J15	Poyle (Heathrow Airport) to Colnbrook (M4)
February 1986	J3–J5	Swanley (M20) to Chevening
October 1986	J19–J23	Chandler's Cross to Bignell's Corner (South Mimms)

A Recipe to Build Your Own M25

If you have ever wondered how difficult it is to build a ring road round a major city, why not have a go yourself by following this simple recipe:

Ingredients:

£1 billion (the EC will give you £5.8 million of
  this, but it won't go very far)
11 years of your life
3.5 million tons of 'black top' asphalt
Over 2 million tons of concrete
33 junctions
11,000 lights
3,000 illuminated signs
234 bridges
284 miles (457 km) of crash barriers
2.1 million new trees and shrubs
39 public enquiries

Instructions:

1. Spend 70 years talking about it with well-paid consultants
2. Plan your route
3. Plan a different route taking account of the several thousand objections that have been upheld by various well-meaning commissions, panels and committees
4. Learn to live with the hatred of everyone who lives within 10 miles (16 km) of your replanned route
5. Appoint lots of builders with experience of building motorways

6. Blame the builders for delays, cost overruns and the inadvertent digging up of Roman artefacts and the bones of Druids

7. Rebury the Druids

8. Do everything the Health and Safety people tell you to do (but no more than that – it is very expensive)

9. Get the prime minister to open the completed motorway

10. Start widening the carriageways before the traffic grinds to a complete halt.

1986

And so it came to pass, by strange coincidence and with perfect symmetry, that the final 3.8 miles (6.1 km) of the M25 were completed by Balfour Beatty between J22 (St Albans) and J23 (South Mimms), 11 years after that same company had built the first, and adjacent, 2.7 miles (4.3 km) between J23 and J24 (Potters Bar).

The complete 117-mile (188-km) ring road had cost £909 million, or £7.5 million per mile, and opened with the capacity to carry 88,000 vehicles per day, a figure that was to prove hopelessly inadequate. It would soon be taking 15 per cent of the UK's motorway traffic on 6 per cent of its motorway network, and so was always destined to age prematurely.

The Not Very Grand Opening of the M25

In the Thatcher era road-building was crucial to the government's plans to boost industry and generate wealth, so the prime minister herself stepped forward to do the honours for the M25, the first politician in a decade who felt proud to open a motorway.

In a low-key but carefully choreographed ceremony somewhere between J22 and J23, on the final stretch to be completed and not far from South Mimms service station, Thatcher took the opportunity to have a go at the negativity displayed by opponents of the motorway, whom she described as those who 'carp and criticise'. She looked one reporter in the eye and asked him whether he could possibly bring himself to describe the M25 as a great engineering achievement for Britain. He subsequently did.

The Department of Transport, who produced a 58-page illustrated brochure to commemorate the opening, had left nothing to chance, right down to a practice run of the removal of a single cone by an employee of similar build to the prime minister the day before. I like to think the employee was made to do this with a handbag swinging from her left arm, which was exactly what happened at the opening ceremony. In fact, Thatcher picked up a cone in each hand and symbolically marched them off to the side of the road. The handbag didn't budge an inch. It probably didn't dare.

Nothing was left behind to mark the exact spot, presumably because it would have been too easy a target for any road protesters still harbouring a grudge about the road's very construction.

Anything for a Day Out

Apparently the people of Norfolk became quite excited when the M25 opened, with many booking up for orbital coach tours with Ambassador Travel of Great Yarmouth. The tours were sold out for months.

1980s

Still in the days before reliable, widespread speed-enforcement devices, supercars were illegally raced round the M25 at night. These time trials were won in under an hour and therefore at average speeds of over 117 mph (188 km/h), including the time taken to stop and pay the toll charge at the Dartford Tunnel.

The M25 Three

In the early hours of 16 December 1988 three men used the M25 to move from one random crime to another, stealing five different cars as they went and committing murder, grievous bodily harm and robbery. Raphael Rowe, Michael Davis and Randolph Johnson, all known career criminals, were subsequently arrested and sentenced to life imprisonment at the Old Bailey in 1990, but their convictions were overturned ten years later, during which time they had consistently maintained their innocence. Two of them admitted to other offences at the time of their trial, but never to the crimes committed around the M25 on the night in question.

Rowe studied journalism on a correspondence course while in prison and since his release

> has carved out a career as an investigative journalist working for the BBC, best known for his work on *Panorama* and in particular for the documentary which contributed in 2008 to the overturning of Barry George's 2001 conviction for the murder of newsreader and *Crimewatch* presenter Jill Dando.

1989

Flying in the face of public opinion, the Thatcher government announced its Roads for Prosperity policy, which it heralded as the biggest road-building programme since the Romans. It planned to implement 500 road schemes, some of which would combine to widen 600 miles (966 km) of existing motorways throughout Britain, including pretty much all of the M25. The inevitable protests followed and many of the schemes were subsequently abandoned in the face of public outrage, including one proposal to widen the M25 to seven lanes in each direction between J12 and J15 (although it has since crept up to six lanes in each direction between J14 and J15 in any event).

1990s

Additional lanes were added in piecemeal fashion but never proved sufficient to cope with increasingly high demand, especially on the stretch that serves Heathrow Airport and links to the M3 and M4 motorways. That stretch was one of the few that the Department of Transport had been allowed to future-proof at the building stage, so they were at least able to make use of the wide central reservation that had been put in place to cater for extra width on each carriageway.

'With this ring road I thee wed!'

In 1991 Chris and Sue Glazier from Kent won a mystery prize in a local radio competition for couples intent on marriage. The prize was a prepaid wedding, which they were told the night before the ceremony would involve spending their wedding night travelling at 50 mph (80 km/h), with their guests being invited to come along for the ride. The couple slept fitfully, possibly dreaming of a trip on the Orient Express, but the wedding the next day at Thurrock Services was followed by a coach trip round the M25. Disappointed as they may have been, the coach had at least been fitted out with a four-poster bed, and the organisers were sufficiently discreet to drop the guests off after the first of three circuits.

1992

Driving a Porsche 911, one driver clocked up a speed of 147 mph (237 km/h), the highest speed recorded by the police on the motorway. Needless to say, he lost his licence.

1993

By now the M25 was carrying up to 200,000 vehicles per day, more than double the traffic levels it had carried when opened just seven years earlier.

1995

First implementation of MIDAS (Motorway Incident Detection and Automatic Signalling) technology on the M25, installed between J10 and J15 to improve traffic flow and reduce the risk of accidents.

1998

William Allen, at the ripe old age of 84, set out to drive the few miles to his daughter's home near Ruislip. Having inadvertently driven onto the M25 at the nearby J16, he spent the next two days going round in circles trying to find the correct exit.

2003

196,000 vehicles were recorded in a single day on the stretch of the motorway closest to Heathrow Airport, between J12 (M3) and J14 (Heathrow).

2005

Completion of the £148-million road-widening project to relieve traffic pressure over the 7.5-mile (12-km) stretch between J12 and J15 and provide access via a new spur road to Heathrow Terminal 5. The motorway was widened to dual five lanes between J12 (M3) and J14 (Heathrow) and six lanes between J14 and J15 (M4). The project won awards for its use of sensitive lighting, low-noise surfacing and recycled materials from the demolition of the old Wembley Stadium two years earlier. The next time you're stuck on this stretch and think it's all over, it is now – but try not to think that you are probably driving over what's left of the iconic twin towers that you didn't want to see demolished in the first place. It just won't help.

2009

The government awarded a Private Finance Initiative contract to Connect Plus to maintain the M25 and the Dartford Crossing for a period of 30 years at a cost of around £6 billion.

2011

According to satnav company TomTom, 29 July saw the longest traffic jam ever recorded on the M25, with a clockwise tailback of up to 49 miles (79 km) between J19 (Watford) and J5 (Sevenoaks).

2011

The first electric vehicle charging 'pump' was installed at South Mimms Services, and more have since been installed at the other service stations on the M25 and more widely on the British motorway network as a whole.

2012

Completion of two widening schemes, at a total cost of £400 million, to create four-lane carriageways in both directions between J16 (M40) and J23 (South Mimms), and between J27 (M11) and J30 (Thurrock). The project came in under budget and in good time for the London 2012 Olympic and Paralympic Games, which had been the intended target.

2012

Coach tours of the M25 were revived by the Brighton and Hove Bus Company, but they petered out after a single summer once the novelty value and press interest had worn off.

2013

On Remembrance Sunday in November thousands of bikers took to the M25 in a clockwise direction from various starting points to salute the country's armed forces and war dead and to raise money for military charities. They all wore red in an attempt to form the largest human poppy imaginable, a moving sight in more ways than one. The event was known as the Ring of Red and has since become one of the annual mass rides put together by the Ride of Respect organisation.

2014

Implementation of Active Traffic Management (ATM), a 'smart motorway' system, in an attempt to ease congestion between J5 (Sevenoaks) and J7 (M23), and between J23 (South Mimms) and J27 (M11). This measure included the latest MIDAS technology as well as conversion of sections of hard shoulder into permanent traffic lanes.

2015

According to the *London Evening Standard* in May 2015, the M25 was now said to handle an average of 170,000 and sometimes up to 250,000 vehicles a day. The Moscow Ring Road still has it beat for the time being, though, with an average of 250,000 vehicles per day.

The General Layout and Goings-on of the M25

> **66** *I didn't come into this to create some reckless, booming economy just within the M25.* **99**

Prime Minister David Cameron, proving that Britain is now considered by many to be divided between the haves inside the M25 and the have-nots without.

THE ROUTE

In the chapters that follow we will start at the Dartford Crossing to the east, at the 3 o'clock position on the M25 clock face, before proceeding clockwise round the motorway. We will travel south through Kent and then westward across the entire width of Surrey. Just south of J13 we will reach the New Runnymede Bridge, the means by which the M25 crosses the Thames for the only time as itself (as we shall see, it isn't quite itself when it crosses the Thames at Dartford). Having enjoyed the briefest of sojourns within Royal Berkshire, we will then re-enter Surrey for one last hurrah before handing over the reins to Buckinghamshire.

At this halfway point, after some 59 miles (95 km) of semi-circumnavigation, we will be in the 9 o'clock position of the M25 clock face. We will then follow the top half of the orbit as it takes us north through Buckinghamshire into Hertfordshire, where it will sweep east to Essex, all the while tracing the route of the Second World War Outer London Defence Ring as it goes. We will cut through the northern tip of Epping Forest before eventually dropping back down to the Essex marshes and, ultimately, the Thames Estuary where we started.

Outer London Defence Ring

The defence ring that the M25 loosely follows to the north of the capital was one of a number of concentric rings of anti-tank defences and pillboxes built at the start of World War Two to halt, or at least slow down, Nazi Germany's planned invasion of Britain.

A combination of natural rivers and man-made ditches up to 20 feet (6 metres) wide and 12 feet (4 metres) deep completely encircled Greater London by the time they were completed in 1940. Some pillboxes and anti-tank defences (mostly concrete cubes, pyramids and cylinders) remain visible within Epping Forest and elsewhere, but we can't see the ditches any more because they have long since been submerged beneath buildings and roads, with many beneath the M25 itself.

WHEN IS A CIRCLE NOT A CIRCLE?

In common with most of Europe and many other countries around the world, Britain refers to circular roads as ring roads or orbital roads; hence the M25 started its (unified) life as the London Orbital Motorway. If the M25 had been built in the USA, it would more likely have been known as the London Beltline, London Beltway or London Loop.

Most orbital roads, whatever they might be called, form complete circles. Strictly speaking, the M25 does not, because the stretch of the orbit that runs between J31 (Dagenham) on the north side of the Thames Estuary and J2 (Dartford) on the south side is in fact the A282, which incorporates the Dartford Crossing tunnels and bridge. To all intents and purposes, though, the A282 is an integral part of the M25 and there is nothing to be gained in excluding it from a book that deals with the history, geography and culture of the entire circular entity, so the A282 is coming into orbit with us as we travel the 117 miles (188 km) of Britain's most infamous motorway together. I would like to be able to tell you that we are about to circumnavigate the longest orbital road in Europe, but I'm afraid the Berliner Ring has the M25 pipped at 122 miles (196 km). At least there was no penalty shoot-out involved in this particular narrow defeat.

WHERE IS THE M25 IN RELATION TO LONDON?

The motorway runs closest to the capital at Potters Bar, 12.5 miles (20.1 km) from Central London, and runs furthest from the capital at Byfleet, an inland island belonging to Woking, 19.5 miles (31.4 km) from Central London.

Watford, close to J19, is the largest town to lie inside the M25, while the little village of North Ockendon, off J29, is the only settlement within the Greater London boundary to poke outside the orbit of the motorway.

Geologically speaking, the M25 is built mostly on sticky London clay, but it does manage to cut itself loose on two occasions to run up and over the chalk hills that have been designated the North Downs Area of Outstanding Natural Beauty: once in Kent, high above the Darent Valley, and once to climb over the Surrey Hills.

The Measure of a King

All radial distances out to the M25 from London are measured (as are all distances from London to anywhere on the British mainland) from the equestrian statue of King Charles I at the top end of Whitehall on the south side of Trafalgar Square. This is not because the statue is sited in the geographical dead centre of London, but because it was originally the site of the final Eleanor Cross built by Edward I to mark the funeral procession in 1290 of his beloved wife, Eleanor of Castile, from Lincoln to Westminster.

In 1647 Charles I replaced this most romantic of monuments – our equivalent of the Taj Mahal, if you will – with the imposing statue of himself. It was just one of the many acts of self-aggrandisement that would lead to his head and torso parting company two years later. Thought about in these terms, it served him right really.

Many people think that distances to and from London are measured from the stone monument that now stands in front of Charing Cross railway station a few hundred metres away on the Strand (I did), but that loose replica of the original Eleanor Cross was actually constructed in 1865 to publicise the new Charing Cross Station Hotel.

THE BEATING HEART OF BRITAIN

At least when it is in full flow, the M25 is akin to the beating heart of the British motorway network, pumping vehicles in and out of the ten major arteries that intersect with it. By linking those arteries together, the M25 provides rapid access from anywhere in the country to anywhere else in the country, via the motorways that radiate out to Wales, Scotland, the West Country, East Anglia, the South-east, the North-east, the Midlands and even the train to France. Even allowing for the fact that the arteries sometimes get clogged, does that sound like the Road to Nowhere to you?

Eight of these ten arteries (the M2, M23, M3, M4, M40, M1, A1(M) and M11) cross over or under to poke inside the M25 to a greater or lesser extent; two of them (the M20 and the M26 in the south-east corner) do not.

Many lesser roads flow in and out of the M25, too – A and B roads that deliver smaller amounts of traffic to the towns and villages that today find themselves dotted around the M25, whether they like it or not. In my more romantic moments (this is a bluff – I derive from the lowlands of Scotland, which means I don't really do romantic moments – but you know what I mean) I think of these A and B roads as tributaries used by the Great River to provide sustenance to those who live within its basin. And before you think I'm getting carried away here, do you think that without the M25 the supermarkets and high streets of the South-east are going to remain stocked in the way we've come to expect? They're not.

THE NORTH OCKENDON QUESTION

As someone who likes things to be neat and tidy, it troubles me somewhat that this little piece of Greater London has been allowed to poke through the circumference of the M25. I therefore urge the good people of North Ockendon to declare themselves independent from Greater London at the earliest opportunity. Their house prices might drop as a result, but I think that is a small price to pay for my peace of mind.

The Communications Act of 2003 got it right already, because it used the M25 as the natural boundary between Greater London and the rest of the country for the purposes of requiring a certain number of television programmes to be made outside of the capital. North Ockendon will probably have its own soap opera within hours of declaring independence. *OckEnders* perhaps?

THE HOME COUNTIES

In completing its journey, the M25 passes through all six of the so-called Home Counties: Kent, Surrey, Berkshire, Buckinghamshire, Hertfordshire and Essex. Most book and website references on the layout of the M25 will tell you that the motorway passes through only five counties, failing as they do to recognise the very short passage across the little bit of Berkshire that manages to infiltrate the circumference just south of J13. I like to think that the good people of Berkshire were just determined to compensate for that dreadful North Ockendon debacle at the opposite end of the orbital.

THE ONE AND ONLY M25 (NOT)

Just in case you thought the M25 was a highly original designation, it is in fact anything but: HMS *M25* was a British warship launched by the Royal Navy in 1915 and scuttled in 1919; the M25 engine powered a Mercedes-Benz racing car in the 1930s; and M-25 is a star cluster in the constellation Sagittarius. M25 isn't even a very original designation for a road, because the Michigan Highway in the USA has been known as the M25 since 1933, as today is the Novorossiysk Federal Highway across the top of the Black Sea in Russia. Since the late 1980s (and about the same age as our motorway, therefore), the M25 has also been a state-of-the-art sniper rifle used by US Army Special Forces and Navy Seals.

OASES IN THE DESERT

I like motorway service stations in the same way that I like railway stations and airport terminals. (Wow, that felt a bit like coming out of the closet, I can tell you!) I know the food isn't always great (although it probably is getting better) and the prices often seem harsh, but I'm a natural-born traveller and people-watcher, and I'm a huge fan of getting to the toilet on time during a long journey.

The M25 has four such oases at which to quench our thirst, rest our weary bones, stretch our tight muscles or do whatever else we need to do to recharge our batteries for the remainder of the journey in hand. These are sited at Clacket Lane between J5 and J6, Cobham between J9 and J10, South Mimms at J23, and Thurrock at J30/31. As we conduct our circular tour of the motorway, we will look in turn at each of these modern-day coaching inns, where one day electric charging points may entirely replace petrol and diesel filling stations, just as these filling stations once replaced smithies and horse feed.

UP AND OVER AND DOWN UNDER

There are 234 bridges under or over the M25, allowing the free and easy passage of other road vehicles, trains, tractors, pedestrians, bicycles and/or horses. At one point there is even an aqueduct for canal boats. The most significant of these bridges, from the point of view of keeping traffic moving on the M25, are the Lyne Railway Bridge, the New Haw Viaduct, the Chalfont Viaduct and the New Runnymede Bridge.

There are only two significant tunnels, the Holmesdale and the Bell Common, but both have stories to tell.

Many of these structures are engineering wonders, and some are more elegant than others. We will pay due attention to them as we go.

THINGS TO SEE AND DO AND THINK ABOUT

Notwithstanding the many fine efforts made to hide away the M25, particularly round its southern semicircle, there are still some fine views to be had of the countryside and of a number of significant buildings and tourist attractions. There are many more invisible ones, sometimes highlighted by the brown tourist signs at the approach to this or that junction, sometimes completely unadvertised and unknown, at least until this book pointed them out. Just knowing that we are crossing from one of the world's hemispheres into another, or passing over the road used by the Romans to conquer Britain, or driving under this cricket pitch or alongside that 'lunatic asylum', can add interest to an otherwise uneventful journey.

Brown Tourist Signs
Courtesy of the French

If you have driven much in France, you will be familiar with the huge, magnificently illustrated brown tourist signs that have alerted us since the 1970s to the next *château*, *abbaye* or *ville historique*. We decided to copycat our Gallic neighbours in the 1980s when we held a trial in Kent of similar but smaller and less elaborate signs, which contained just words and simple pictograms. There was a simultaneous trial in Nottinghamshire of even less elaborate signs with mere words, but the pictogram version won the day and an increasing number of them have been popping up on our roads ever since.

There are surprisingly few brown tourist signs on the M25, given the number of tourist attractions that lie within and without its circumference, so either Highways England is charging too much for the privilege, or tourist attractions don't think there is much of a market amongst those who circle the capital. Those who do advertise their wares on the orbit have some serious attractions to offer, from Hampton Court Palace to New Wembley Stadium, from Waltham Abbey to Chessington World of Adventures. We will touch upon them all as we complete our circular (and probably rather circuitous) tour of the motorway.

SAFETY FIRST

As motorists, we expect two things when we set out on a journey: to get from A to B in a reasonable timescale and to arrive safely at B. Believe it or not, those expectations are entirely compatible with the objectives and actions of Highways England, but the odds are rather stacked against them in the case of the M25. With so many vehicles pounding the tarmac day in and day out, managing traffic flow and maintaining the surface is never going to be easy. It is also a thankless task: the press went to town when a pothole across three lanes caused a tailback in 2014, but we never stop to reflect how on earth the highway people mana keep the surface so smooth 99.99 per cent of the time, or how they manage to keep that much traffic flowing freely and safely at all. We probably don't even care that much, but here are some of the reasons that might just calm us down a little when the going gets tough:

Smart Motorway Technology

The MIDAS (Motorway Incident Detection and Automatic Signalling) technology first installed on the motorway in 1995 applies variable speed limits automatically, taking account of traffic movements, incidents and weather monitored by electronic sensors. The system relies on all drivers heeding the advice given in order to improve traffic flow and reduce the risk of accidents, but of course most of them do no such thing and they probably won't until hefty fines are regularly imposed by the system for breaking the variable limits (which are already mandatory, as opposed to advisory, in some places). In the meantime, many drivers will continue to shoot themselves in the pedal by disobeying the limits and then blame everyone but themselves for the resulting stop–go effect on their progress.

The ATM (Active Traffic Management) system first installed in 2014 included the latest MIDAS technology as well as the conversion of sections of hard shoulder into permanent traffic lanes (with refuge areas at regular intervals taking the place of the hard shoulder for breakdowns). The opportunity was also taken to introduce 'stealth cameras' to catch motorists travelling at over 70 mph (113 km/h). Painted grey instead of the previous eye-catching yellow, they are difficult to spot high on the gantry, especially against a grey sky, and they caught 700 speeders within their first two months of operation. These cameras can even scan across lanes (conventional speed cameras have to be trained on a single lane), so changing lanes before driving under the next gantry will no longer save us. We have been warned!

Traffic Patrols

The Highways England traffic officers we see around the motorway in high-visibility 4x4 patrol vehicles work alongside the Kent, Surrey, Thames Valley, Metropolitan, Hertfordshire and Essex police forces to manage and clear road incidents. We can tell them apart because their Battenberg markings (so called after the Battenberg cakes they resemble) are black and yellow, as opposed to the blue and yellow equivalent of police cars (or the green and yellow of ambulance vehicles or the red and yellow of fire and rescue vehicles). It is an offence to ignore the instructions of any traffic officer, whatever colour of German cake they might be driving.

These traffic patrols will do everything they can to keep the traffic moving, including the use of rolling roadblocks, which means we are welcome to join the slow-moving procession behind them as they keep out front until they reach the piece of debris that has been reported lying on the carriageway. In the style of a Formula One safety car, they will then move aside as the impatient feet of the motorists behind simultaneously hit their right-hand pedals. We're off!

The police officers in particular can also move a bit when they have to. In March 2015 two Surrey Police BMW 350s responded within three minutes to reports of a red Ferrari California doing 150 mph (241 km/h) near J8. The Ferrari was pulled over and the driver arrested before J10.

Control Centres

If we lift one of the SOS phones between J1 and J15 on the southern M25, we will get through to the Highways England control centre at Godstone near J6. If we lift one of the phones between J16 and J31, we will get through to the control centre at South Mimms near J23. They will know exactly where we are and may even home in on us by CCTV while we are talking to them. There is a separate control room for the Dartford Crossing, on the south side of the river.

Using information supplied by the sensors of the smart motorway system, in addition to live CCTV camera feeds, the officers in these control centres also advise motorists through the electronic signs mounted above or to the side of carriageways that, for example, there is an incident ahead which has effectively closed one of the lanes, requiring drivers to proceed with caution at a lower-than-normal speed.

Breakdown Services

According to the AA, the most-asked question on its online route planner is 'How can I avoid the M25?' but it doesn't prevent that organisation alone from attending about 18,000 incidents on the M25 each year (about 50 a day). The AA also reckons that there are a greater number of 'serious' breakdowns on the M25 than on any other motorway in Britain, largely because drivers ignore warning lights on their dashboard in the desperate attempt to get to Gatwick, Heathrow, Luton or Stansted in time to catch a plane. But that is nothing compared to the madness of the motorist who stopped on the inside lane of the motorway to ask an AA patrolman for directions while he was fixing a vehicle on the hard shoulder, or the driver who stopped her car on the outside lane when the fuel warning light came on – according to the Surrey Police officers who attended the 'breakdown', she was confused because it wasn't the car she usually drove. She probably just thought, 'Better safe than sorry, I'll just park up here until I can get some more petrol delivered'.

Accidents Will Happen
(but most of them don't need to)

There are hundreds of road accidents every year on the M25, as there are on all British motorways, and it is reckoned that about nine in ten are caused by driver error as opposed to mechanical failure. Statistics provided in recent years by www.safermotorways. co.uk suggest that accidents are caused on a regular basis by drivers doing one of the following stupid things whilst driving at speed:

→ Making telephone calls

→ Texting or emailing

→ Accessing social media sites

→ Over-celebrating when they hear their team score a goal on the radio

→ Falling asleep

It is estimated that we have to take our eyes off the road for less than two seconds to veer off course or smash into a slowing or stopping vehicle in front of us. I have been trying to think of an acronym to describe **M**obile **O**perators **R**ound the **O**rbital **N**etwork, but it just won't come to me.

In December 2014 a particularly tragic accident between J25 and J24 caused a long tailback after two Sudanese asylum seekers who had been hanging from the undercarriage of a lorry all the way from Calais became too cold to hang on any longer and tried to escape to the grass verge when the lorry got stopped in stationary traffic. One of them made it. The other became trapped between the rear wheels as the lorry moved away, and suffered fatal injuries. Unaware of the reason for the delay, as we usually are in such circumstances, motorists in the tailback complained bitterly on social media and of course blamed officialdom and the inadequacies of the motorway as they bleated on about how dreadful their own lives had been made on that particular day.

Some motorists sink to pretty low depths even when they know that an accident has happened, as evidenced by the prosecution of over 40 drivers who all slowed down to take photos or videos of the emergency services' attempts to cut a lorry driver free from the wreckage of his truck one morning in June 2015.

Emergency Services

The emergency services are in attendance around the M25 all too often, and usually when the road is at its busiest and therefore at its most dangerous; but just occasionally they will sneak on when no one is looking. If a section of road is closed overnight for repair or widening or cleaning, and there is a spare piece of road not being worked on between the junctions in question, they will stage critical incident exercises that would have the effect of blocking the motorway if they happened for real, thereby leaving themselves better prepared for the real incidents they do have to contend with.

Keeping the Show on the Road

Closures and diversions can sometimes be the bane of a motorist's life, but we should perhaps try to bear in mind that most of the work being carried out is in fact for our benefit and that very often it is motorists themselves that are the cause of the work that needs to be done. Highways England usually need to repair crash barriers because bad driving has caused accidents that in turn caused vehicles to hit them, and they have to widen carriageways and renew tarmac and replace bridge expansion joints and all manner of other things because of the insatiable demand of the human being to travel, not because there's anything in it for them particularly.

The demand for more and more lanes on the M25 in particular has been staggering since the day it opened in 1986 with three lanes on each carriageway. Now there are four, five and even six lanes on each side, and we continue to fill them. It is little wonder that there are often more than 20 lots of roadworks going on simultaneously at various points around the motorway.

Some of the less obvious maintenance jobs that Highways England have to carry out on a regular basis include the pruning of vegetation along the verges and the cleaning up of litter which has been thrown from vehicles, spilled from waste-disposal carriers, or just dumped on the hard shoulder or verges of the carriageway. Some bizarre items have appeared during the dead of night, including a table tennis table.

Driver Location Signs

These enigmatic yellow-and-blue signs by the roadside are set at 500-metre intervals and are for use by the control centres and emergency and breakdown services to pinpoint the location of an incident, and for drivers who have broken down to report their exact position.

The yellow writing on the blue background displays the number of the motorway, the direction of travel (on the M25, this is A for clockwise and B for anticlockwise) and the distance in kilometres from a designated starting point (in the case of the M25, this point is near junction 31 on the north side of the Dartford Crossing). So a location marker pinpointing a spot on the anticlockwise carriageway of the M25 situated 172.6 km from junction 31 will look like this:

M25
B
172.6

It is not entirely clear to me why these measurements are conveyed in kilometres when all other distances on UK motorways are expressed in miles. If I ever find out, I will start work immediately on *M25 – The Sequel*.

Pollution Control Valves

You will see signs for these all round the M25 and have probably spent hours pondering their purpose. Ponder no more, for they are used to close off the motorway's drains in the event of a chemical or fuel spill and prevent such spillage from reaching the surrounding countryside, where it would pollute plant life and endanger wildlife.

Knocking Our SOX Off

The M25 is illuminated by more than 10,000 streetlights during the night to help reduce accidents. The road started life with old, yellow low-pressure sodium lighting (since you ask, the technical term for this is SOX), but that has now largely been upgraded to clearer, high-pressure sodium lighting (since you ask again, the technical term for this is SON).

'Well, that's 118 years of my life I won't be seeing again!'

Official road traffic figures provided in early 2011 for the calendar year 2010 showed that the average time taken to cover the distance between J16 and J23 of the M25 had increased from 17 minutes to 22 minutes. One national newspaper thought it would be useful to extrapolate this information and explain to the motorists affected that together they had endured delays amounting to over one million hours, or 43,000 days, or 118 years, and that they had therefore been stranded for longer than a whole lifetime. If you use the M25 regularly and sometimes feel as if you're spending your entire life on it, apparently that's because you are.

Mind the Gap

On 14 November 2014 a 16-foot (5-metre) stretch of road caved in because it had failed to set properly after being repaired during a night of heavy rain and flood alerts. This left a foot-deep pothole on the anticlockwise carriageway at J9 near Leatherhead, causing the closure of three lanes and a 12-mile (19-km) tailback for two hours. That morning the head of the AA showed a distinct lack of imagination and a penchant for overdramatisation by dusting down the 'road to hell' analogy for the press and demanding an investigation. Minister of Transport John Hayes jumped on the bandwagon and similarly demanded an investigation to determine the cause of the tailback. If such an investigation took place, it probably found that a section of concrete had failed to set overnight in heavy rain. My invoice is in the post.

Squiggle-free Traffic Signs

The typeface used for motorway signs in the UK is a sans serif, which is French for 'without any squiggly bits', and the font used is known, perhaps unsurprisingly, as Motorway. This font comes in two weights: Motorway Permanent (used on the regular white-on-blue direction and distance signs); and Motorway Temporary (used on the black-on-yellow roadwork signs).

The typeface was designed in 1958 by British graphic designers Jock Kinneir and Margaret Calvert, who also designed the non-motorway signs in the UK, including many of the pictograms that we are so familiar with, such as the instantly recognisable Men at Work. The design duo also produced the signage that is used on the UK railway networks and at UK airports, so we are probably more familiar with their work than we could possibly have imagined.

It is a simple, no-fuss typeface designed to be read at speed from a distance, hence the huge size of the signs and the absence of distracting squiggly bits. It is a design so good that there has been no need to change it in over 50 years.

M25 TRUCKERS

For a long time it seemed that most lorries on British motorways belonged to the ubiquitous Eddie Stobart or his French and German equivalents, Norbert Dentressangle and Willi Betz. Nowadays, there is such a proliferation that truck stops around the M25 have become increasingly multilingual venues. Drivers who overnight in their own 'Three Pedals Hotel' are providing freight and logistics services on behalf of thousands of companies from dozens of countries across Europe. They may have driven their curtainsiders, container artics, rigids or lowloaders to the orbital from as far away as Sweden, Portugal or even Turkey.

In addition to the four service stations on the M25 that are available to us all, truckers can also choose from more traditional greasy-spoon pit stops like the Truck Stop at Waltham Abbey (off J26) or the Titan Truckstop at Lakeside (off J31).

THE FIVE BEST TOWNS TO LIVE IN
AROUND THE M25

If by now you are feeling inspired to live as close to the motorway as possible, here are the five best towns to live in around the M25, at least according to the results of a newspaper poll in recent years, taking account of green space, crime levels, schools and transport access (in addition to being handy for the M25, they are all within 30–45 minutes of London by train):

➜ Sevenoaks, Kent

➜ Wallington, Greater London

➜ Beaconsfield, Buckinghamshire

➜ Harpenden, Hertfordshire

➜ Ware, Hertfordshire

Focus, people!

According to a study by campaign group Transport Focus in 2015, the M25 has taken on mythical status amongst drivers who have never used it and probably never will. Apparently, these drivers consider the motorway to be intimidating on account of its aggressive drivers, and confusing because their heads would get muddled trying to cope with so many lanes and with the clockwise and anticlockwise terminology used to describe the directions of the carriageways.

There are, however, some fine examples of people who just will not be intimidated by a large circular motorway, like the family who decided to keep going, and going, and going until they found the sign for Newcastle (I'm not sure whether they're still on the M25 or not) and the elderly lady who had to be rescued by police while cycling the wrong way in the slow lane near Godstone in Surrey.

M25 PLAYLIST

Just one more thing before we set off on our circular tour of the UK's most infamous motorway – should we find our temper fraying at any time because we have been held up, or because we're just not in the mood to be driving in the first place, here are a few road-related suggestions to start us off on a playlist that is guaranteed to cheer us up on any road trip, even on the M25:

→ 'Drive'   The Cars

→ 'Mustang Sally'   The Commitments

→ 'Road to Nowhere'   Talking Heads

→ 'Born to Run'   Bruce Springsteen

→ 'Chasing Cars'   Snow Patrol

→ 'Start Me Up'   The Rolling Stones

→ 'Born to Be Wild'   Steppenwolf

→ 'King of the Road'   The Proclaimers

→ 'Hotel California'   Eagles

→ 'Bohemian Rhapsody'   Queen

→ 'The Chain'   Fleetwood Mac

→ 'Bright Side of the Road'   Van Morrison

→ 'I Drove All Night'   Cyndi Lauper

→ 'Home'   Edward Sharpe and the Magnetic Zeros

→ 'Cars'   Gary Numan

Just in case you don't know, the Steppenwolf offering was used on the iconic soundtrack of the 1969 counterculture road movie *Easy Rider*, the Queen number gained additional notoriety as the in-car head-banging singalong song in the 1992 American comedy movie *Wayne's World*, and the Fleetwood Mac track is the one that has been used for years in the introduction to Formula One TV coverage.

The Bit That's Not the M25 At All

"One way or another, we are now getting the road system that Britain needs."

Pathé News broadcast on the opening of the first Dartford Tunnel in 1963

As I touched upon earlier, the stretch of the orbital that runs from just north of J31 on the Essex side of the Thames Estuary to J2 on the south side of the river is in fact the A282 trunk road. It is named Canterbury Way and incorporates both of the Dartford Tunnels and the Queen Elizabeth II Bridge. In other words, this stretch is not motorway at all and that explains why all the road signs are green for a while, as opposed to motorway blue.

The Dartford Crossing is measured at 1.8 miles (2.9 km), and the total length of the A282 including the crossing is 5.2 miles (8.4 km), all of which are included in the 117 miles (188 km) that the M25 is said to cover.

Because the A282 includes junctions 31, 1a and 1b, it makes the M25 something of a rarity in having three of its junctions on somebody else's road. For the sake of motoring convenience, these three renegade junctions are nonetheless counted amongst the 33 that the M25 is always said to have.

THE HISTORY OF THE DARTFORD CROSSING

1936–38

The drilling of a pilot tunnel began, but work was soon interrupted by the Second World War.

1959

Work on the original tunnel was finally resumed. The intervening 20-year gap allowed much better drilling technology and ventilation systems to be used.

1963

The first Dartford Tunnel opened with one lane in each direction. It carried about 12,000 vehicles a day (about 4 million a year, as opposed to the 2 million that had been forecast). The toll was half a crown (two shillings and sixpence, or 12.5p in modern parlance), which is roughly the purchasing equivalent of £2 today.

1980

The second Dartford Tunnel opened on the east side of the original to cope with increasing demand, thereby creating two lanes in each direction.

1986

The tunnel access roads on both sides of the river were linked to the new M25.

1988

Ownership of the crossing was transferred from Essex and Kent County Councils to Dartford River Crossing Limited, a private company. The Dartford–Thurrock Crossing Act declared that no tolls would need to be paid beyond 2002.

1991

After three years of construction, the Queen Elizabeth II Bridge opened to the east of the tunnels. It was 450 feet (137 metres) tall and 1.8 miles (2.9 km) long, and was at the time the longest cable-stayed bridge in Europe. It was also the first bridge to be built to the east of the capital since Tower Bridge in 1894. The Dartford Crossing now had four lanes in each direction, as both tunnels were now used for northbound traffic only, with the bridge correspondingly dedicated to southbound traffic.

2000

A new Transport Act declared that tolls would continue to be charged beyond 2002.

2003

It was announced that all ongoing charges would henceforth be known as charges, not tolls, thereby keeping the government's original promise that no tolls would be paid beyond 2002. Genius.

2008

Night-time charges between 10 p.m. and 6 a.m. were abolished.

2014

The free-flow, number-recognition Dart Charge system (which replaced the earlier DART-Tag attached to windscreens) was introduced to avoid long queues at tollbooths. As with the London Congestion Zone Charge, motorists are expected to pay in advance or by midnight the following day. Reductions were applied for registered account holders, e.g. if we registered our car, we would pay £1.67 as opposed to £2.50 per crossing.

2015

The tollbooths were demolished, resulting in fewer delays and faster crossing times. Traffic figures by now had reached 50 million vehicles a year (an average of

137,000 a day, with up to 160,000 vehicles on the busiest days).

VIEW FROM THE BRIDGE

On a clear day we can see a long way south towards the North Downs and a long way west towards the London skyscape that includes Canary Wharf and The Shard. Immediately below us are the container ships, tankers and all manner of other vessels that line up at the deepwater berths on both sides of the river here. There are also countless storage tanks and distribution centres, containing everything from oil, aggregates and industrial chemicals to supermarket products and chilled goods, sitting alongside line after line of shiny new cars that arrive here in their thousands by ship from the Continent, via the port of Zeebrugge. Everything looks matchbox size from the top of the bridge, but the one thing we can't look down on from up here is the large, thin chimney of the Littlebrook Power Station on the south side just a little bit to our right as we drive across, because at 705 feet (215 metres) it is way higher than we are.

BIG BUSINESS

The other thing we might notice on both sides of the crossing is a large number of hotels. Apart from being rather handily placed to break car journeys within Britain or to and from nearby Continental Europe, they are also used extensively by businesses large and small for meetings, conferences, summits, training conferences, lunches and whatever else businesses need to get together to do with each other. The main reason for the popularity of these hotels in this respect is that, thanks largely to the M25, they are easily accessible from all parts of the country and beyond, and are not exactly hard to find either (just look for the bridge supports from 9 miles out if you're coming from the north). So the next time we need to do some blue-sky thinking or run a few ideas up our corporate flagpole or storm our collective brain, we should set our satnavs for the Dartford Crossing.

As we can get here by car in under an hour from the Eurotunnel terminal in Folkestone, it is apparently not that unusual for Jürgen or Amélie to pop over to one of these hotels for a quick meeting with Tom, Dick or Harriet (please note the politically correct version of this saying, which I have decided to establish as a more appropriate norm for the twenty-first century).

Stay Where You Are, Bob!

Nestling by the Thames in the shadow of the bridge are Tesco and Unilever distribution centres on the north side and extremely visible Asda and Sainsbury's centres on the south side. They are but four of the many dotted around the M25 for obvious reasons. If you ever wondered where your I Can't Believe It's Not Butter comes from, it's the Unilever storage and distribution centre in the shadow of the QEII Bridge. Well, it could hardly have come from a cow if it isn't butter, could it?

The next time we find ourselves lamenting the number of lorries on the M25 (or any other motorway, for that matter) we should perhaps try to bear in mind what would happen if the lorries across Britain suddenly stopped rocking and rolling. It has been estimated that if they didn't leave their yards or distribution centres for between one and two weeks, the country would by then have come to a standstill. There would be no food in our shops and no supplies in our hospitals, our manufacturing would have ground to a halt and, without fuel, our traffic would be at a complete standstill (except maybe for old Bob and his wife Doris, because they hadn't had the car out these last two weeks, but they'll soon run out of petrol as well).

DARTFORD TUNNEL CYCLE SERVICE

When the first tunnel opened in 1963, the Department of Transport commissioned five unusual double-decker buses to give pedestrians and cyclists a free ride through the tunnel. The bottom deck was cut out to provide racks for 23 bicycles accessible from either side, with an extra space at the back for tandems and prams. The humans themselves took the one straight staircase up to the top deck, where they enjoyed splendid views of the tunnel roof for the duration of the journey.

The service ran every six minutes but soon proved to be loss-making, so the buses were decommissioned and replaced by Land Rovers with trailers. Today the service is similar, but with just a cycle carrier on the back of a Highways England vehicle and sometimes longer waiting times, while pedestrians have been dropped from the scheme altogether.

DARTFORD CROSSING MONEY-SAVING TIPS

Here are my top tips to save lots of money when crossing the River Thames at Dartford:

1. Cross as a cyclist at most times of the day or night. You won't actually be allowed to cycle, but you will be invited to hop on board the complimentary shuttle service mentioned above.

2. Buy a motorcycle and have as many free rides as you like all day, every day.

3. Drive your car back and forward as often as you can between 10 p.m. and 6 a.m. every night.

4. For even bigger savings, buy a multi-axle truck and drive backwards and forwards as many times as you can between 10 p.m. and 6 a.m. every night. I

reckon you could save at least 16 x £6 a night if you really put your mind to it, allowing for one quick toilet break at Thurrock Services at around 2 a.m. I have extrapolated these figures to calculate that, if you make 16 crossings every night for a year, you would save £35,040. You would then be well on the way to being able to afford your second multi-axle truck and the more trucks you add to your nightly crossings, of course, the more you will save.

5. This one is more a tip about how to cope better psychologically with the charges than a tip about how to save money (see 1 to 4 above) or about how to grow a trucking business (see 4 above). In any event, just do what I did a couple of years ago and take your car to Denmark on holiday and then drive to Sweden across the Øresundsbron (the Oresund Bridge, the one that has featured in the most excellent Scandi-drama *The Bridge* in recent years). This will cost you 94 euros (£68) for the return trip and will leave you feeling much better when you come home and pay just £2 to use the Dartford Crossing. I now think of the Dartford Crossing charge as really good value for money, and you too can develop a positive attitude like mine simply by driving to Sweden and back.

Note: I should perhaps point out that the business case for tip number 5 is not quite watertight. Given the high cost of food and drink while you are in Denmark and

Sweden, not to mention the aforementioned bridge toll, you will have to spend some time getting over that financial hit before you start to feel good about the relative cheapness of the Dartford Crossing.

European Route E15

As if the A282 did not have enough of an identity crisis as an unofficial part of the M25, it is conversely but quite definitely a part of the E15, one of the European roads within the International E-road Network developed by the United Nations Economic Commission for Europe. The E15 runs north–south over a distance of 2,230 miles (3,590 km) from Inverness in Scotland to Algericas on the Bay of Gibraltar at the southern tip of Spain. In common with all UN-designated E-routes, it has no roads of its own, so it simply borrows everyone else's like the road-surface parasite it is. Between J24 (Potters Bar) and J1b (Dartford), it leeches itself onto the M25, including, therefore, the entire stretch of the Dartford Crossing.

The UK recognises the idiocy of the United Nations by not bothering to display any of its E numbers, but many of us are familiar with the confusion caused by many of our

European neighbours, who continue to display them alongside their own national A-road numbers. Uzbekistan, as you might expect, stands alongside the UK in having nothing to do with them. The next time we find ourselves travelling along the stretch of road that is the A282/Dartford Crossing/Canterbury Way/E15/M25(ish), we should spare a thought of solidarity for our Uzbek comrades in the ongoing struggle against complete and utter nonsense.

↑ Kent (J1a–J5)

Once we are off the QEII Bridge, we start our orbital journey by travelling down through Kent, the Garden of England, although we are so close to the western edge that we are probably on the patio as opposed to the lawn.

The stretch that takes us down to J5 in the bottom right-hand corner of the motorway sits in prettier countryside than we might think from behind the wheel. We're just not allowed to see it all. We will run parallel to the line of the Darent Valley, home to the eponymous river which rises to the south of Westerham in Kent before winding its way north to spill itself into the Thames Estuary just west of Dartford. In doing so, we will cut through the Area of Outstanding Natural Beauty that incorporates the chalky North Downs and many pretty villages, all of which are easily accessible, if not exactly visible, from the motorway.

It is because the building of the M25 was not allowed to interfere with such outstandingly natural beauty (left to its own devices it would have done, but conscientious objectors won the day) that we must complete this north–south stretch some way to the west of the valley. Denied the flatness of the valley below between junctions 3 and 5, we must therefore go up and over the North Downs, so if you ever wondered why we had to climb a long way up to junction 4 before dropping back down to junction 5 (or vice versa, travelling anticlockwise), wonder no more.

You're probably now thinking, the next time I go up and over the M25 here, I really must pay more attention to the wonderful views from on high. Well, no, you won't. If the M25 had been allowed to go over the very top, we would indeed have enjoyed some magnificent views, but because going over the top would have offended the eyes and ears of those privileged enough to live or enjoy rambling in the valley below, the builders were made to cut deep into the chalk and the M25 must forever keep itself to itself around these parts, unloved and unlit, for it is one of the rare stretches of the motorway to be denied lighting. But all is not lost, for it is always possible, as we shall see, to leave the motorway to enjoy an area's hidden treasures.

Once we turn west after J5 towards Surrey, we will enjoy much finer vistas as we look north to the escarpment of the North Downs we have just left behind.

THE FUNCTIONS OF THE JUNCTIONS

Let us first, however, have a look at the functions of the junctions on this south-east stretch of the motorway:

Junction 1a – Littlebrook Interchange

Start the clock

With the Thames behind as we set off southwards in a clockwise direction from 3 o'clock, we soon find ourselves at J1a, which takes its name from the nearby power station with the towering chimney (there used to be five such chimneys in a row at that one power station, but the energy companies have been made to cut down on their smoking these days).

Strictly speaking, as we have seen, this is in fact J1a of the A282, the bit of the M25 that isn't the M25 at all.

Junction 1b – Princes Road Interchange

The original Dartford Tunnel junction

This junction pre-dates the M25 as it was originally built in 1963 to serve the first Dartford Tunnel. It was very important at the time as the intersection with the A2, but it is now the primary exit for nearby Dartford. Note the east–west bridge for pedestrians and cyclists above as you drive under the giant roundabout that was built to carry Princes Road over the motorway.

Junction 2 – Darenth Interchange

Next stop: Canary Wharf

This junction takes its name from the River Darent, as do the nearby Darenth Country Park, built on the grounds of the former Darenth Asylum, and Darenth Valley Golf Club. They all insist on adding the 'h' at the end reportedly because a nineteenth-century cartographer once spelled the Darent Valley incorrectly as the Darenth Valley and lots of people have been copying the error ever since (although the Darent Valley itself now seems to be largely silent on the 'h' front).

Here the motorway crosses over the A2, which runs in a pretty straight line all the way from London to Dover on the Kent coast. It is a major commuter artery into London past the O_2 arena (see 'Places to Visit') and through the Blackwall Tunnel, a stretch of road I used for many years as part of my drive from home in East Sussex to my workplace at Canary Wharf, and I can tell you that it has a tendency to become a little congested during the rush hour (for effect, I have used the literary ploy of understatement here). Since 2007, this junction has also served the thousands of motorists travelling daily to catch the Eurostar train service from its station at Ebbsfleet.

The Bluewater Experience

Whatever their original or intended purposes, junctions 1a, 1b and 2 of the M25 now also serve to deliver up to 13,000 carloads of people at a time to the nearby Bluewater Shopping Centre. Opened in 1999, the triangular centre designed by renowned architect Eric Kuhne sits in beautifully landscaped grounds in an old chalk quarry. Each point of its triangle houses a department store approached by a grand boulevard lined with chestnut trees (John Lewis), lime trees (Marks & Spencer) or oak trees (House of Fraser).

People do not just go there to shop, though; they go to eat, drink, meet friends and family, catch a film or simply people-watch. It is enjoyed by many as an entire day out, an alternative to Margate, an opportunity to be part of a vibrant city scene where it never rains, an escape from whatever people feel the need to escape from. Catering for more than 25 million visitors each year, it has become such a part of British culture that it now features on the national curriculum for geography!

Junction 3 – Swanley Interchange

Gateway to Europe

It can take less than an hour from this junction to the check-in booths at Folkestone for Le Shuttle, the train that will take us and our car through *le tunnel sous la Manche*. Therefore, in as little as 2 hours after joining the M20 at junction 3 of the M25, we can be driving through France, with the whole of Europe at our wheels.

Taking the slip road after the one that leads to France will allow you to make the rather more parochial journey into nearby Swanley, which isn't very French at all, but it does at least give its name to a junction of the M25, which is more than can be said for France. Swanley 1 France 0.

This junction also serves the A20, another major (and often clogged) artery into London if you travel north-west until you reach New Cross in the London Borough of Lewisham. Taking the A20 in the other direction will, just like the A2, deliver you all the way to Dover. As it runs pretty much parallel with the M20 as far as Le Shuttle terminal at Folkestone, just think of it as the slow road to France from J3.

Bridging the Gap

After the stretch of road from J2 to J3 was completed in 1977, there was a gap of nearly ten years until the motorway continued through and beyond J3 on its southbound journey through Kent. They did manage in 1977 to build the concrete bridge that would carry the motorway over the M20 here, but it was left unconnected at either end, just sitting up there in the sky minding its own business for almost ten whole years. The singing satirist Richard Stilgoe once sat up on the endless bridge playing his piano and singing a ditty for the BBC's *That's Life* programme. His ditty was called 'Bridge over Troubled Mortar', which turned out to be truer than he could possibly have imagined, because while he was recording up top the Kent CID were digging in the concrete below for the remains of an assassin named Nino Ricci, who, ironically, had probably managed a few more hits than Richard Stilgoe ever did.

Road-rage Killing

In 1996 notorious criminal Kenneth Noye stabbed 21-year-old Stephen Cameron to death following a road-rage incident on a slip road at junction 3. Noye fled to France and then Spain, but was later caught, extradited and sentenced to life imprisonment.

Junction 4 – Hewitts Roundabout

Go west!

In keeping with the policy to keep the M25 away from the Darent Valley to the east, the slip roads on J4 exist only on the west side, providing access to and from a number of the towns and villages that nestle hereabouts in the south-east quadrant of Greater London. The slip roads on and off the motorway are situated comfortably within Kent but the only way to reach anywhere in Kent when we come off here is to travel west into Greater London on a long spur road and then double back from the Hewitts Roundabout that gives the remotest part of the junction its name, after the adjoining Hewitts Road and nearby 'pick-your-own' Hewitts Farm. The roundabout that sits above the motorway itself, and which allows us to enter and exit the carriageways, shall forever remain nameless.

Junction 5 – Chevening Interchange

Keep out!

The M25 does a strange thing down here at its bottom right-hand corner: it connects itself to itself by means of a slip road, known to the road-building world as a TOTSO (Turn Off To Stay On). It is the cause of many a bottleneck exacerbated by the arrival of the M26 at this same point. The main reason for this nonsensical layout was the successful campaign of the good burghers of Sevenoaks to the south to keep the motorway well away from their doorstep, leaving the planners to do their best with the confined space they were given to the north. And the resulting design didn't just make it difficult to stay on the M25; it made it difficult to get off as well, because it left out the bits of road that would have allowed north–east, east–north and east–south traffic flow. Half-a-job Harry was here.

This all adds to a personal prejudice I have held against Sevenoaks since my early teens, when I was put off geography for years after being forced by a dull geography teacher to study the even duller subject of crop rotation in the Sevenoaks area. To this day, whenever I am stuck in a bottleneck at junction 5, I damn the harvests of the fields that lie to the south, and console myself with the fact that the residents there lost six of their seven eponymous oak trees in the great storm of 1987. I've lost count of the number of times I've been stuck in a traffic jam just north of One Oak, I can tell you. [Note for residents of Sevenoaks: I'm only kidding, except for the bit about not really caring about your crop rotation.]

As we shall see in the next section, the junction takes its name from the nearby Chevening Estate.

ON THE ROAD (J1A–J5)

Now we know what the junctions are for on the Kent stretch of the motorway, let us go back and look at what we can see from the road itself. The surprises in store include an igloo and an elegant bridleway.

Romans and Pilgrims

As we pass under the second of the two road bridges between J1a and J1b, we are ducking under Watling Street, built over a distance of 276 miles (444 km) by the Romans in AD 47–48 to allow themselves free and easy passage from Durovernum Cantiacorum (Canterbury) to Londinium, Verulamium (St Albans in Hertfordshire) and Viroconium Cornoviorum (Wroxeter in Shropshire), where they stopped to orgy a bit before invading Wales.

This same route became popular with pilgrims on their way to Canterbury in the centuries that followed the death of Thomas Becket in 1170, as encapsulated by Chaucer in his *Canterbury Tales*, so we really are passing under the line of one of the most important routes of both ancient Britain and the England of the Middle Ages. If you're a historian, you probably salivate all the way from J1a to J1b, and who can blame you?

Polar Huts

There is a huge, strange-looking, brown igloo-like structure to be seen on the J3 roundabout, one of ten dotted around the motorway to store thousands of tons of rock salt mined in Cheshire for the gritters to use in winter.

High-flying Horses

Halfway down the chalk slope between J4 and J5 we drive under the most elegant of bridges, which takes the form of a straight line on top of a single wide arch embedded high in the chalk face on either side. It is part of a bridleway that runs through Pilots Wood (above us on both sides) so keep your eyes open for the odd high-flying horse or two.

Chevening House

Best seen to the north from the anticlockwise bend at J5, Chevening Estate hosts one of the most important buildings in the country, the official residence of a Cabinet Minister appointed by the Prime Minister or a descendant of George I. More often than not this has been the British Foreign Secretary, although Prince Charles did once nab it for six years under the George I rule. The stunningly impressive house dates back to the early seventeenth century and, while strictly off limits to the public, it is possible to get a close-up view if we visit the gardens, which are opened to us plebs three times each year in support of local charities.

Sadly, it became a timeshare operation in 2010 when the realities of coalition government literally hit home and Foreign Secretary William Hague was made to co-exist there with Deputy Prime Minister Nick Clegg. There are 115 rooms at Chevening, however, so if one of them wanted to play loud music and the other wanted an early night, they could do both. That's why it's called 'coalition' government.

More High-flyers

We can work out the position of Chevening Estate by following the line of the high slender flyover that straddles J5, now part of the Chevening Road that runs between Chipstead in the south and Chevening in the north. The two villages depended on one another long before the M25 came along, because the population of Chipstead used the school and church in Chevening; so to preserve their interdependency the narrow flyover was built over the A21, which itself was built over the M25, which in turn was built over the M26. As we pass underneath, we can try to imagine high-flying dignitaries on the way to Chevening House alongside some high-flying small residents of Chipstead on their way to school.

Outstandingly Beautiful (and that's official)

Travelling south to J5, we can't see the North Downs for the chalk, but we then drop below the escarpment and head west on a bed of clay towards the border with Surrey. This means we can now enjoy many fine views as we look north to the Area of Outstanding Natural Beauty we have just driven through, albeit while blindfolded at the time by steep banks on either side of the carriageways.

PLACES TO VISIT (J1A–J5)

From the pretty villages of the Darent Valley to the old stomping grounds of Anne Boleyn, Winston Churchill and Wolfe of Quebec further south, we are truly spoiled for choice if we decide to use this stretch of motorway as a gateway to the England of old. In the case of Chartwell (Winston Churchill) and Hever Castle (Anne Boleyn), brown tourist signs will point us in the right direction from the motorway. But we will start with the London of today:

O$_2$ Arena

Use J2 to head straight west along the A2 until you reach the iconic building that started life as the Millennium Dome before becoming one of the largest and most successful entertainment complexes on the entire planet. Go there to enjoy its many bars and restaurants or its 11-screen cinema complex or its wintertime ice-skating rink, or to take in a sporting event like the annual ATP World Tour Finals tennis tournament in the autumn or one of the many shows performed by the world's top music stars. The myriad superstars to have graced the arena include AC/DC, Beyoncé, Bob Dylan, Lady Gaga, Michael Bublé, Prince, The Rolling Stones and Britney Spears, who still holds the all-time attendance record at the arena (all ten of her shows there have sold out within 30 minutes).

Darent Valley Path

If we're feeling a bit tired and stiff after taking in all those shows at the O_2, we could really stretch our legs by walking or cycling the entire 19 miles (30.4 km) of this long-distance path, all the way from Sevenoaks to the River Thames and within the shadow of the M25 for most of the time. If we do, we will be rewarded with views of hop vines, rolling hills, pretty meadows and picturesque riverside villages, not to mention a wildfowl reserve, some significant Roman leftovers and some very fine public houses. If it's the wonderful sight and fragrance of lavender we're after, we can come in July and pretend we've gone to Provence for the day.

If the whole path sounds a bit too much, there are lots of manageable chunks to be had between pubs, railway stations or villages along the way, and if we really can't be bothered with any of that walking from A to B stuff, we can just drive through the pretty countryside instead and park up for a stroll in any one of the villages, including the four I'm about to tell you about.

Eynsford

An award-winning village near J3 with an award-winning pub, Eynsford's little humpback bridge over the river has featured on many a biscuit tin and chocolate box, but we don't have to use it to cross the river. We could instead party like it's 1899 and pretend our car is an ox and cart as we drive through the shallow ford that lies in the shadow of the humpback. In 1994 the village starred in its own six-episode television programme, a fly-on-the-wall documentary called *We're a Snooty Lot: 20 Miles from Piccadilly*.

There is also a relatively complete (as ruins go) early Norman enclosed stone castle on the outskirts.

Lullingstone

Leave at J3 and choose from Lullingstone Country Park to picnic under its ancient trees, Lullingstone Roman Villa to see what you can do with a few hundred thousand mosaic tiles when you put your mind to it, and Lullingstone Castle to follow in the footsteps of once-regular visitor Henry VIII (you will be particularly adept at this if you have gout).

Lullingstone Castle has the added attraction of the intriguing World Garden of Plants (as seen over 12 episodes on BBC2 in 2006 and 2007), a concept dreamt up by plant-hunter Tom Hart Dyke (Lullingstone Castle is his ancestral home) while he was serving his time in 2000 as a kidnap victim in the jungle that straddles Colombia and Panama. Time well spent, as it turns out, but it probably didn't seem that way at the time to Tom Hart Dyke.

Shoreham

Accessible from J3, J4 or J5, this traditional riverside village with pubs to match also hosts an aircraft museum in tribute to the brave airmen who won the crucial Battle of Britain in 1940. It was the most bombed village in the UK during the Second World War once the Luftwaffe got wind of the fact that many of the area's splendid manor houses had been commandeered by the British Army.

Otford

This village to the north-east of J5 boasts some fine medieval buildings, the only roundabout in the UK to enjoy listed status (on account of the duck pond in the middle of it), and an outdoor model of the solar system – built to scale, as you might reasonably expect.

Quebec House

Use J5 or J6 to get to Quebec House in Westerham, for this was the birthplace and childhood home of General James Wolfe, hero of Quebec in 1759 when he was fatally wounded after scaling the Heights of Abraham with 3,000 men and a couple of cannons to defeat the French against all the odds and secure North America for Britain. He was only 32 at the time but had been in the army since he was 13, so he was no rookie. The splendid Georgian home, now a National Trust property, is full of artefacts and exhibits about the young general's life and career.

Chartwell

Carry on now to Chartwell, the nearby home of Winston Churchill and his wife Clementine from 1924 until his death in 1965, following which it too was handed over to the National Trust. The red-brick country house has been preserved pretty much as it was when the great statesman, war leader and historian lived there, and the hillside gardens and wooded trails are a delight. We can even visit the garden studio where Churchill liked to sit and paint, but I should perhaps warn you that he was a far better statesman, war leader and historian than he was a painter.

Hever Castle

If Tudor homes and portraits are your thing, travel a bit further south from J5 or J6 to find this childhood home of Anne Boleyn. You will find the calming walks around the beautiful gardens, lakes and mazes especially poignant if you have an extra finger on your right hand or a particularly slender neck.

Surrey
(J6–J12 and J14)

On this stretch of the motorway we will cross the dividing line between two of the planet's hemispheres and on many days of the year, if we get our timing right, we will be treated to spectacular sunsets as we drive due west (or, of course, as we look in our rear-view mirrors travelling east).

We will cover a distance of 36 miles (50 km) in travelling from Clacket Lane service station on the Kent/Surrey border to the point at which Surrey hands over to Buckinghamshire at J14. We will often be able to see large chalk quarries to the north as we make our way along a line that often runs parallel with the North Downs Way.

We will feed and be fed by the junctions that service two of the world's most important airports, and we will witness the longest slip road in the country as we once more climb over the chalk hills of the North Downs to satisfy the demands of the objectors below. Towards the end of this chapter of our journey, we will enjoy the briefest of flirtations with Royal Berkshire before Surrey completes its handover to Bucks.

The places that this stretch of the motorway provides access to include royal palaces, horticultural wonders, thrilling adventure parks and five racecourses.

THE FUNCTIONS OF THE JUNCTIONS

Junction 6 – Godstone Interchange

Eastbourne, here we come!

If you're about due to retire, head south from this junction on the A22 and before you know it you will be promenading along Eastbourne Pier, but don't forget to take all your belongings with you. I'm all for spur-of-the-moment, life-changing decisions, but you have to remember that Eastbourne is a big commitment. You can check out any time you like, but you can never leave. Feel free to enjoy one last fling as you pass by Lingfield Racecourse on the way (there is a brown tourist sign that you can follow from J6, whether you are on your way to retire in Eastbourne or not), and make sure that you enjoy the Ashdown Forest on your way down.

As its name suggests, the more immediate function of the junction is to serve the pretty village of Godstone to the south, which offers up timber-framed buildings, two conservation areas, a nature reserve, a lovely village pond and a bit of the North Downs Way.

Junction 7 – Merstham Interchange

Four-leaf clover

This free-flow junction is one of three four-level road stacks on the M25. We are on the bottom level as we pass under, looking up at the other three levels as we go. The M23 running north–south (and thereby forming a giant cross with the M25) is the one way up top, 75 feet (23 metres) above the M25, and it crosses up and over this intersection for a distance of 1.5 miles (2.4 km) in order to achieve the required height and still land softly on the other side. Woven through the air in between these two giant trunks, the slip roads form the shape of a four-leaf clover within a diamond outline (known, in fact, as a 'cloverleaf interchange' to those who design such things). From the air, which is another way of saying 'using the aerial view on Google Maps', one can but marvel at the symmetry achieved by the designers and engineers alike.

Before I forget, though, in all the excitement of the intersection's symmetry, I should also tell you that this is the junction that serves London Gatwick Airport just 9 miles (14 km) to the south on the M23. But if flying is not on your mind, you can just stay on that motorway until it becomes the A23 and eventually takes you all the way into Brighton. If you do this in the summer months, I should warn you that you will need to queue for a parking space for about three weeks, by which time the kids will really be doing your head in, and then spend £5 million for each hour you spend in one of their multi-storey car parks. Do it in the middle of a cold, wet miserable day in November, though, and you will only have to queue for about two hours. This time of the year has the added advantage that the sea air out on the pier will be much more bracing and therefore much better for you. I should be a travel agent, really.

Nearer to home, this junction takes its name from the nearby village of Merstham, which has a small art gallery containing works by many fine artists including Henry Moore and Joan Miró, no less.

London Gatwick Airport

It might be London's second-busiest airport, but Gatwick can still handle up to 55 flights an hour on the world's busiest single-use runway (its second runway is only ever used as an alternative to the main one). Almost 40 million passengers passed through one or other of its two terminals in 2014, the most popular destination being Barcelona, followed by Malaga, Dublin and Amsterdam, while Edinburgh was the most popular UK destination. EasyJet accounts for almost half of the passengers using Gatwick, but British Airways also has a strong base there.

Junction 8 – Reigate Hill Interchange

Record-breaking slip road

This humble junction has a real claim to fame, because it possesses the longest motorway slip road in the country. The clockwise off-slip here climbs up Reigate Hill for 1.5 miles (2.4 km) before finally reaching the roundabout at the top, exhausted but with the satisfaction of a job well done.

The junction largely exists to serve the communities of nearby towns like Reigate and Banstead but, perhaps surprisingly, the A217 that crosses over it will take us all the way to the Fulham end of the King's Road if we head north, and all the way to Gatwick Airport if we head up and over Reigate Hill and continue south on a line parallel with the M23. This could be useful to know if the M23 to Gatwick is ever clogged up good and proper, while it's never a bad thing to end up on the King's Road in my view.

Junction 9 – Leatherhead Interchange

Double trouble (1)

This mile-long junction is a bit of a mess. It consists of a complex roundabout at either end of a long squiggly slip road (the old Leatherhead bypass) that sort of runs parallel with the motorway, except it has to pass underneath it at one point so that it can serve both carriageways in both directions. I hope that has helped to clear things up for you.

I have family living off this junction, my mum in Ashtead just north of the M25 and my brother and his family in Leatherhead just to the south. After years of trying to get to grips with J9 in order to visit them, I still get confused. At one point it got so bad they didn't see me for five years. How I get confused depends on whether I am wearing my clockwise or my anticlockwise head (and, of course, the direction I am actually travelling in as I approach the junction). On one occasion I rejoined the motorway not long after leaving it and ended up back at J8 before I could turn round and have another go at J9. Apparently, it only takes five minutes to drive from my brother's house to my mum's flat, but I think that assumes you don't get on the M25 at any stage during those five minutes.

It doesn't help here that we are denied any physical bearings, which is down to the fact that the road was submerged below high embankments in order to mitigate disturbance to those living in the area. When this stretch was widened to four lanes in the mid nineties, an extra 550,000 trees and plants had to be grown so as not to offend the eyes and ears of any residents who would otherwise be within sight or earshot of the carriageways. My mum and my brother's family tell me they are grateful, but always with less conviction than I would ideally like to hear.

Having said all that, this junction does provide access to some jolly useful places, like Epsom Downs and its famous racecourse, home each June to the Derby and the Oaks, the most famous flat races in the calendar. It is also a favourite junction with children of all ages, because if we follow the helpful brown tourist signs from

J9 they will take us to Chessington World of Adventures (more of which later). Or we can take the A24 and head straight down to the coast, for this is another road that heads direct to the English Channel from the M25. This time our destination will be Worthing and its seaside pier.

Junction 10 – Wisley Interchange

Anyone for tennis? Or rowing? Or horseracing? Or football?

After the recent trauma of J9, I am happy to report that this is a nice, straightforward three-level junction that exists to intersect with the splendid A3 trunk road. I say 'splendid' for two reasons. In one direction it will take us south-west through a huge swathe of the beautiful South Downs National Park and all the way on to historically important (from a naval point of view) Portsmouth. In the other direction it is London's most free-flowing artery and will deliver us to the sporting splendours of Sandown, Wimbledon, Putney and Fulham.

Sandown Park is home to the Group 1 Eclipse Stakes horse race in July. Wimbledon is home to the biggest and best tennis tournament the world will ever know. When the AA road signs for Wimbledon Tennis go up on either side of J10 in the summer, we know it's time for strawberries and cream. Putney nestles gorgeously by the stretch of the Thames that is home to top rowing clubs and bears witness each year to the university boat race. On the other side of the river, just upstream, lies Craven Cottage, the old red-brick-fronted football stadium of Fulham FC, the one that looks as if Roy of the Rovers still plays there (and, goodness knows, Fulham look as if they could do with signing him following their recent fall from the heights of the Premier League).

The village of Wisley that the junction takes its name from might look small to the naked eye, but it does in fact punch way above its weight in hosting two large heathland commons, a golf course, a stretch of the River Wey and the headquarters and gardens of the Royal Horticultural Society (see 'Places to Visit' below).

Junction 11 – Addlestone Interchange
Smarten yourself up a bit

This is a straightforward junction built for the purpose of feeding traffic to and from the towns that lie around and about, like Chertsey to the north, Woking to the south, and the Georgian town of Weybridge to the east. Nearby Addlestone, which gives its name to the junction, is home to the Crouch Oak, a tree said to be 800 years old. We can also find our way from this interchange to the Thorpe Park theme park and the Brooklands Museum of aviation and motor racing (see 'Places to Visit' below for more information about both).

You might want to wash your car and make a bit of an effort with yourself while you're about it if you're thinking of going into Weybridge, though, because it's well posh – so posh, in fact, that in a survey conducted a few years back it was found to have six of the ten most expensive streets in the whole of the South-east. At least comb your hair anyway.

Woking has a couple of interesting claims to fame, as the home base of the McLaren Formula One team and as the site of a Martian tripod. I don't think Martians have actually landed in Woking; the tripod is there simply to commemorate the fact that H. G. Wells wrote *The War of the Worlds* while living there. At least, that's what the Martians who live in Woking now would have us believe.

Junction 12 – Thorpe Interchange

The carpet beater

Given this junction serves only to link the M25 with J2 of the M3, the design employed looks somewhat convoluted, a bit like a carpet beater with handles on all four sides (apparently the technical term for such a junction is a turbine or whirlpool interchange). And once we get off the M25 onto the M3, we're going to be stuck on the latter for a while, because it is some way north-east before we can get off it at J1 and some way south-west before we are given the opportunity to alight at J3.

I assume they called this junction the Thorpe Interchange because Thorpe Park lies right beside it on the east side, but we can't actually get to Thorpe Park from Thorpe Interchange (we have to go north to J13 or south to J11 for that), so they might want to rethink that when they get a moment.

If we do head south on the M3, it will ultimately take us down through Hampshire most of the way to Southampton. As motorways go, it's a scenic one, and we can stop off to admire the cathedral city of Winchester on the way down. If we take the M3 in the opposite direction towards London, it will deliver us via the A308 to Kempton Park racecourse, a particularly useful thing on Boxing Day each year, for that is the day on which they run the King George VI Chase. If we carry on a bit further along the A308, we will come to Hampton Court Palace (see 'Places to Visit' below). If, instead, we just carry on until we drop off the end of the M3 and then carry on in a straight line, we will soon enough come to Twickenham Stadium, home to the Rugby Football Union and England's home matches in the Six Nations Championship in February and March each year.

Junction 13 – Runnymede Interchange

Flirting with royalty

J13 straddles the borders that separate Royal Berkshire to the west, Surrey to the south and Greater London to the east. Although the junction does provide access to Thorpe Park and Runnymede within Surrey, most of the significant places it leads to, like Windsor Castle and Royal Ascot, are within Royal Berkshire. We will therefore return to J13 in the Royal Berkshire chapter.

Junction 14 – Poyle Interchange

Well-earned promotion

Taking its name from the nearby industrial and agricultural area of Poyle, this junction started life as just a roundabout but hit the big time when it inherited a trumpet spur (you get to be called this if your spur has a loop at one end) as part of the widening works required to service Terminal 5 of Heathrow Airport. The junction also serves Terminal 4 and we need to follow different signs from the off depending on which of the two terminals we want. If we're on cargo business, we need to stick with the Terminal 4 guys initially.

The interchange actually sits at the point where Surrey, Buckinghamshire and Greater London seem to come together to say a brief hello, but the area is so dominated by Heathrow and its traffic that it probably doesn't really matter where we are in relation to the rest of the world. In any event, this is pretty much where the M25 starts the handover from Surrey to Buckinghamshire. It will run along the border between Buckinghamshire and Greater London for a couple of miles or so, i.e. in a sort of no man's land between J14 and J15, before the baton is finally in Buckinghamshire's hand just after J15.

Off the original roundabout (i.e. ignoring the trumpet for a moment) we are offered one brief opportunity to head west away from Heathrow, in the direction of Windsor and Eton. If we take this minor route, we will soon pass the Queen Mother Reservoir to our right. I knew she liked a drop of water with her malt, but I had no idea she drank that much.

ON THE ROAD (J5–J14)

We have had a thorough look at the purpose of the Surrey junctions, and now it is time to go back and see what lies in store for us as we drive that stretch of the motorway. This being the only county on the motorway to contain two service stations, we should at least be able to keep our caffeine levels high.

Indeed, the first thing we come to after we pass over from Kent into Surrey between J5 and J6 is Clacket Lane Services, one of the largest motorway service stations in Europe. To check it out, take the slip road after the irritating NOW FULLY OPEN sign that has been there for longer than anyone can remember, probably since the services first fully opened over 20 years ago. Somebody needs to change that sign to STILL FULLY OPEN AFTER ALL THESE YEARS.

Clacket Lane Services
Addressing the issues
Sitting on both sides of the motorway just below the North Downs between J5 and J6, this ranch-style Roadchef service station was opened in 1993. With an appalling lack of attention to the detail of the spelling, the services were named Clacket Lane after Clackett Lane, a country road that passes over the motorway just before the clockwise entrance.

The services suffer from a bit of a geographical identity crisis, not only on account of the missing 't' in their name, but also because they happen to sit on the Surrey side of the Surrey/Kent border, whereas their nearest postal town is Westerham, which is of course in Kent. If the idea of quite correctly addressing a letter to someone in Westerham, Surrey excites you (and why wouldn't it?), I suggest you write to the manager at Clacket (sic) Lane Services. While you're about it, tell him about that irritating sign at the entrance to his service station.

Coining it in

A Roman road running north–south, along with a small temple, were discovered during the archaeological surveys that preceded construction of the services on both sides of the motorway. Roughly speaking, we drive over it heading clockwise just before the petrol station, or at the entrance to the Coach and Lorry Park when heading anticlockwise. The road once led (I'm guessing during Roman times) from London to Lewes and served the great ironworks in the Sussex Forest. Some Roman artefacts uncovered during the excavations are on display in glass cabinets on both sides of the motorway, but these are unfortunately situated between the entrances to the gents and ladies toilets, so there is a half-decent chance of getting arrested on a public indecency charge if you linger too long at either end of the cabinets. 'Honest, officer, I'm writing a book about the M25 and I wanted to tell my readers all about the splendid pieces of porcelain on display outside the ladies toilet' was the speech I found myself preparing just in case.

Good food (and that's official)

In common with most motorway service stations around the country, if not the world, Clacket Lane doesn't always get the best press, so you can imagine how pleased they were in 2009 when Lord Adonis, the then Secretary of State for Transport, paid them a surprise visit and declared that he had enjoyed a good meal. I don't want to detract from a 'good' rating for motorway food, but I have found it difficult since the end of the eighteenth century to take seriously the view of any man who calls himself Lord Adonis, so best decide for yourself.

Time travel

Travelling clockwise, Clacket Lane Services is our last chance to freshen up or have a coffee before leaving the world's Eastern Hemisphere, because we are now only about two minutes from crossing over to the other side of the world. If we are travelling anticlockwise, this is our first chance to freshen up or have a coffee since leaving the world's Western Hemisphere about two minutes ago.

At the exact point we travel across the Prime Meridian Line, which is about 1.5 miles (2.4 km) west of Clacket Lane Services, we will rather excitingly be travelling through time, or at least through the point at which the world's time begins, which is nearly the same thing. If we are travelling clockwise, and are willing to believe that time travel is a perfectly realistic proposition, this is where we are most likely to find ourselves travelling back in time. It's probably still not that likely to happen, but your kids don't need to know that.

Unfortunately I seem to be the only person who cares about knowing exactly where the M25 crosses the Prime Meridian Line, so it's going to feel a bit unceremonious until I can convince the powers that be to do something about it. I haven't actually tried yet, and I might never get round to it either, but just in case there is a power that be reading this book, I think you need to put a sign up here saying 'The Western Hemisphere Welcomes Careful Drivers' (and an equivalent sign on the other side of the motorway, of course).

Up and over again

On our way up to J8 we climb the Surrey Hills portion of the North Downs to reach the highest point of the M25 at 705 feet (215 metres). The road digs deep into the chalk here, just as it did the last time it had to climb up and over the North Downs above the Darent Valley in Kent, and for the same reason – local objections to the unsightliness and noise of a motorway on the doorstep. We must be neither seen nor heard by this part of the Home Counties until we are over the Surrey Hills, at which time we will once more be allowed out to play.

Cobham Services

Opened by Extra Motorway Services between J9 and J10 in 2012 at a cost of £75 million, this new kid on the service-station block is already handling over 60,000 vehicles and 90,000 customers a day. Its design is ultramodern, bright and spacious, resembling that of an airport terminal, and it has all the usual retail and business facilities on site, along with a 24-hour self-service launderette and the increasingly standard electric-car charging points. It is one of the easier service stations to get in and out of or, as their own website puts it, there is 'convenient ingress and egress for all routes', which is always useful to know if you're thinking of turning up there in the nineteenth century.

The services are situated pretty much halfway between Gatwick and Heathrow Airports, one of the main reasons they were considered necessary, and after all it is one of the busiest sections of the motorway, where motorists often need to take a break from the frustrations of slow-moving traffic. It also greatly reduces the considerable 63-mile (101-km) gap that previously existed between the services at Clacket Lane on the south side and South Mimms on the north. There are those, however, who think that services are not really needed on an orbital motorway in the first place, because the general idea is to get on and off the orbit in as short a time as possible. The local authorities and residents around these parts took just such a view and protested long and hard against the development, which is probably why it took a staggering 19 years to get from the drawing board to the grand opening.

Fun and Games

Las Vegas-style slot machines abound in twenty-first-century service stations around Britain and beyond, and the M25 ones are no exception. Indian and Thai princesses, goddesses of the Amazon, Mexican amigos, Irish leprechauns and 'pig wizards' will all try to lure us in with the promise of gold or the guaranteed luck of the Irish. I wouldn't mind some gold myself, especially if a goddess of the Amazon was signed up to deliver it to me, but I couldn't help but wonder how weary a traveller would have to be to get lured in by a 'pig wizard'.

The only thing that disturbs me more than the pig wizard are the unnecessarily large illuminated posters of TV and radio broadcaster Noel Edmonds, towering above the machines in that alluring way he has of tempting people into a darkened room to deal or no deal their money away.

But then it came to me in a flash. The pig wizard and Noel Edmonds must be part of a government-run scheme to scare people away from the evils of gambling. It certainly works for me.

New Haw Viaduct

About halfway between J10 and J11, which are less than 5 miles (8 km) apart, we will cross over the engineering marvel that is the New Haw Viaduct. This will not be immediately obvious to us, but we can tell from the low fences to the side of the carriageway, the quick one-two that our wheels make as they cross over the bridge joints, and the National Grid electricity pylons that pass overhead at one end.

The reason for these eight spans of road sitting on seven giant concrete legs for a distance of some 940 feet (285 metres) is to allow the M25 (and us with it) to cross over the London to Woking railway line and the River Wey Navigation some 980 feet (300 metres) below. This is also the point where the Wey Navigation (the first of three canals on our orbital journey) intersects with the Basingstoke Canal just south of the Thames, so if we could get out and look over here, we would be treated to a very watery view indeed. My recommendation, however, is that you remain seated for the time being and visit the surrounding area when a more suitable opportunity arises.

Lyne Railway Bridge

Just before J12 clockwise stands the first concrete, cable-stayed railway bridge in Europe, the remarkable (but far from pretty) Lyne Railway Bridge, suspended by cables reaching down from two 98-foot (30-metre) supports that are sunk into the central reservation. This unusual design was used primarily because the railway line had to cross the motorway at a seriously skewed angle. The trains that cross here are travelling between Virginia Water and Chertsey on the Chertsey Branch Line that was built in the nineteenth century off the main London Waterloo to Reading line, which itself passes under the M25 between J12 and J13.

Shepperton Studios

These famous studios, now part of the mighty Pinewood Studios empire and still boasting 15 stages, lie not far to the east of J12. Hundreds of great films have been shot there since the studio's beginnings way back in 1931, including *Lawrence of Arabia*, *The Omen*, *Blade Runner*, *Gandhi*, *Out of Africa*, *Four Weddings and a Funeral*, *Notting Hill*, *Love Actually*, *The Da Vinci Code*, *Gladiator*, *Gravity* and two of the *Star Wars* films. Intriguingly, I will be returning to the filming of *Four Weddings and a Funeral* when we get to J31.

There are no studio tours to be had here, but we can at least imagine ourselves in the latest blockbuster to while away the time on this notoriously slow section of the motorway. I now do a pretty good Daniel Craig and a more than passable Dustin Hoffman.

The Future is Art Deco

Just before J13 on our right travelling clockwise (but with a much better view travelling anticlockwise) is Future House, the building that houses Future Electronics, a worldwide company that specialises in electronic components distribution. It somehow manages to look simultaneously art deco and space age, a result not at all unpleasing to the eye in my view.

'Water, water, everywhere, and every drop to drink.'

Just after J13 the motorway takes us between two of the six huge man-made reservoirs that provide London with its water supply, having siphoned it off from the nearby Thames in the first place. The one we run closest to on our left (easily identified by its uniform raised bank) is Wraysbury Reservoir and the one over to our right beyond the trees is the King George VI Reservoir. The latter was finished in 1939 but was left empty for the following eight years due to the outbreak of war; it is said that a mock Clapham Junction Railway Station was built inside to confuse Luftwaffe bombers. If I saw a giant railway station inside an empty reservoir, I would be confused too.

We might spot sheep on the banks as the water company maintains a population of them to keep the grass down and thereby make it easier to inspect the water; and we might also spot some of the birdlife supported by the network of reservoirs around these parts (more of which later in the 'Natural World' chapter).

Extended Rush Hour

The M25 is generally at its busiest between J12 and J16, not least because of the number of people who need to get to and from nearby Heathrow Airport. These include air travellers, airport and airline workers, delivery drivers, freight hauliers, coach drivers, passenger picker-uppers and passenger dropper-offers, and maybe even the odd plane-spotter. The rush 'hour' tends to drag on for about three hours in the morning and about four hours in the late afternoon and evening. This is all particularly stressful if we have a plane to catch and we didn't leave enough time for our journey, or if we left plenty of time for our journey but then suffered a long delay as a result of an incident caused by some other driver who got a bit stressed trying to catch a plane. Forgive me if this sounds a bit obvious, but you really do need to build in a huge amount of contingency if you are travelling between these junctions and need to be somewhere by a certain time. If you need to use the M25 in order to catch a plane yourself from any of the London airports, you need to allow even huger amounts of contingency or, better still, stay overnight at an airport hotel if you possibly can.

PLACES TO VISIT (J6 TO J14)

Reigate Hill, Gatton Park and Box Hill

Just off the south side of J8 we will find the National Trust area of Reigate Hill and Gatton Park, popular with walkers, picnickers, kite flyers and butterfly spotters. Reigate Hill commands fine views over the Weald to the south, whereas the adjoining Gatton Park runs downhill to the valley below on the North Downs

Way. Gatton Park is full of unusual trees, gardens and ponds, designed in the eighteenth century by the famous landscape architect Lancelot 'Capability' Brown.

Similarly stunning views over the Weald are to be had from nearby Box Hill (just off J9), where the National Trust even provides a purpose-built viewpoint just a couple of hundred metres from their car park and restaurant/shop.

Chessington World of Adventures

This resort just off J9 started life as a zoo in 1931 and added a theme park in 1987. The zoo is still going strong, with over a thousand animals plus a sea life centre, and the theme park is jam-packed full of rides to excite children of all ages, including adult ones. It includes themed areas such as Forbidden Kingdom and Land of the Dragons, roller coasters such as Scorpion Express and Vampire, and the most popular ride of all, Rameses Revenge, which includes a high-speed, upside-down head soaking. Apparently, the ride was responsible for the busiest year in the park's history after it opened in 1995. Who knew that what the public wanted all along was to have their heads soaked upside down at high speed? It seems that Chessington World of Adventures did.

RHS Garden, Wisley

Follow the brown tourist signs from J10 to find the UK's second most popular garden after the Royal Botanic Gardens at Kew. The Royal Horticultural

Society planters have done themselves proud here, as their offerings include a huge glasshouse with separate desert, tropical and temperate climates, a fruit field, a rock garden, an alpine meadow, a wild garden, a walled garden and probably every other garden you can think of. There's even a national heather collection if you're an expat yearning for the Scottish Highlands.

The Inland Island of Byfleet

Just to the east of the motorway between J10 and J11 lies the strange anomaly that is Byfleet, an outpost of Woking situated on an inland island on account of the fact that it lies between the River Wey to the west and the River Wey Navigation (canal) to the east. The Wey Navigation now belongs to the National Trust and can be accessed from many points within the 'island'. The River Wey runs parallel to the M25 for quite a long stretch, as the river flanks the clockwise carriageway for a few miles. As we noted earlier, the M25 at Byfleet is at its furthest point from Central London, thereby giving the 'islanders' an additional claim to fame.

Just to the north of this medieval village (but still on the 'island') is Brooklands, the former aerodrome, aircraft-manufacturing facility and motor-racing circuit, the last of which was famous for its steep 'wall of death' banks. The site now houses a museum to both aviation and motor racing, including a large collection of vintage cars, motorbikes and planes. They even have a Concorde that was partly built at Brooklands in the first place, back in the 1970s. Also on site is Mercedes-

Benz World, which has over a hundred cars on display and which gives driving lessons to anyone over 1.5 metres (4 ft 11 in) tall, allowing children several years short of the legal driving age to have a go on the original Brooklands race circuit.

Thorpe Park

Just off J12 but only accessible from J11 or J13, as we have also already noted, Thorpe Park is right up there with Chessington in the excitement stakes. Brown tourist signs are again on hand to lead us to some of the fastest and scariest roller coasters known to mankind.

Try Saw – The Ride if you want to drop from a great height at a 'beyond vertical' angle: the published rules say that you can only go on this ride if you have a maximum 51-inch (130-cm) torso restriction. I guess if you're the sort of person who worries what that even means, you're probably not the sort of person who is going to want to do the 'beyond vertical' thing anyway. You could always just try the Colossus instead, as that is pretty much limited to a straightforward vertical loop – it then adds a cobra roll, a double corkscrew and a quadruple barrel roll, I assume as some sort of warm-down exercise. Then there's the Swarm: if you're the kind of wimp who is happy to dawdle along at 60 mph (97 km/h) in a forward direction while suspended in mid-air, then fine: choose one of the easy-peasy, forward-facing seats for babies. If you're not that big a wimp, do the same ride on one of the seats that faces backwards at the rear. Otherwise, I'll call you a baby again.

If you get a bit hot and bothered after a while on the coasters, I suggest you cool off on the Tidal Wave ride. That will calm you down no end, I should think.

Hampton Court Palace

Just follow the brown tourist signs up the M3 towards London from J12 to arrive at one of the most famous tourist attractions in the entire universe. In addition to wandering around the magnificent splendour of the palace and grounds with your jaw dropped and your eyes popped out, you will also get to see some truly great art from the royal collection, including works by Canaletto (long since a favourite of the British royal family) and Rembrandt. You will be struck dumb by the vastness of the Tudor kitchens responsible for turning Henry VIII into a bit of a porker, marvel at the sumptuousness of the Great Hall and the Royal Chapel, and admire the grand indoor courts where real men used to play real tennis (as opposed to the pretend lawn tennis played nowadays). You will probably have even more fun trying to find your way out of the most famous maze in the world – unless you don't, of course, in which case you'll starve to death. It has been said that over a hundred tourists are lost in the maze each year and that there is a secret tunnel to take their bones away so as not to frighten other visitors, but I'm not sure if that's true or not.

Runnymede

Take off in the direction of Windsor from J13 to find this thought-provoking National Trust gem and its memorial to Magna Carta. Everyone knows that this is where naughty King John reluctantly sealed the Magna Carta 800 years ago, in 1215, and that parts of the document remain the basis of democratic governance all over the world today. We can provoke our thoughts yet further by visiting the nearby memorials to the Commonwealth Air Forces and to John F. Kennedy, the latter sited on an acre of land donated to the USA in 1965. In the spirit of Magna Carta, we will find no border controls in place as we approach the memorial.

Today the surrounding area may be home to rock-star royalty and Russian mafia, but here where it matters the Thames still laps gently and we can still get away from it all to put our troubled world to rights, at least in our own heads. King John would even today feel at home amongst these meadows, reed beds and ancient woodlands, and he would almost certainly recognise the 2,500-year-old Ankerwycke Yew not far across the river (whether, as many historians believe, that was where he sealed the Magna Carta or not). But he would also be in for a bit of a shock if the royal barge took him not very far downstream on the river to see and hear the M25 thundering over the New Runnymede Bridge above him. Would he or would he not consider that we had made some real progress in his absence? Discuss.

The M25 flirts with Berkshire briefly at J13 just as it crosses the Thames. In fact, as I mentioned in the last chapter, Berkshire, Surrey and Greater London all appear to bump into each other at J13, but I have awarded it to Berkshire because it is the only junction to truly serve the county.

Royal Berkshire, to give it its full title, is the only royal county to exist within the UK, having been elevated to regal status as a sort of 'thank you' for hosting much land belonging to the Crown, including Windsor Castle, the royal palace that the Queen considers her home.

THE FUNCTION OF THE JUNCTION

Junction 13 – Runnymede Interchange

Flirting with royalty

Roundabouts on either side of the Thames, and therefore on either side of the junction, allow clockwise and anticlockwise traffic to access the A308 towards Windsor, even if the clockwise traffic does have to perform some rather elaborate moves in the process.

The interchange gets it name from the fact that the motorway has only just crossed the Thames on the New Runnymede Bridge.

ON THE ROAD (J13)

New Runnymede Bridge

The New Runnymede Bridge over the River Thames at J13 was specifically built for the M25 in 1983 and has since been widened to six lanes in each direction, plus an extra two lanes to carry the southbound traffic of the Staines bypass (part of the A30). The separate red-brick bridge that runs alongside it on the west side, it seems with only inches to spare, was part-designed by Sir Edwin Lutyens in the 1940s and carries the separate northbound carriageway of the A30.

The new bridge of 1983 was itself a rebuild of an earlier bridge completed in 1961, so strictly speaking the New Runnymede Bridge should really be referred to as the New New Runnymede Bridge. The new, new bridge follows the same aesthetically pleasing design of the original Lutyens bridge, with a low, wide single arch on each of its parallel concrete frames, and in that regard the architects and engineers were congratulated for their sympathetic design and building work. If they had really cared, though, they would have found a way to cover the obscene concrete of the new, new bridge with a red-brick wall akin to the one that Lutyens designed, or at least they would have found a way to create the illusion of such a facade.

Archaeologists had a field day when the excavation for the New Runnymede Bridge took place, finding much pottery and many bronze objects from a Late Bronze Age riverside settlement that lurks beneath the surface (honestly, there are so many advantages to building motorways that it makes you wonder why we don't have lots more).

PLACES TO VISIT (J13)

Windsor Castle

Join the million other people who visit each year to see what 39 successive monarchs have done with the place since William the Conqueror knocked it up as a wooden fort on this most commanding of hilltop positions a thousand years ago. Admire the glorious State Apartments and their many treasures; the 1:12 scale doll's house, complete with electricity and hot and cold running water, crafted by Sir Edwin Lutyens in the 1920s for Queen Mary; and St George's Chapel, home to the tombs of Henry VIII and his favourite wife Jane Seymour, as well as that of Charles I, who was buried here after his head had been sewn back on.

The devastating fire that laid waste to over a hundred rooms in 1992 gave meaningful employment to Europe's finest craftsmen for a while and the result was a palace restored to its former glory in five unbelievably short years, which just goes to show what can be done when you put your top people in charge of a project.

If Windsor Castle ever comes on the market, though, the one thing you might mention to get the price down a bit is the number of jumbo jets flying over it all day, every day. Whoever thought to build a medieval castle that close to a busy motorway and an international airport should get bow-and-arrowed for their trouble.

Windsor Great Park

This is effectively Windsor Castle's 5,000-acre (20-square-kilometre) front garden, having evolved from its original purpose as a royal hunting forest into the magnificent park it is today, stuffed full of ponds and lakes, ancient oak trees, sweeping vistas and an impressive deer population. The prominent Snow Hill, the one with the copper equestrian statue of George III on top, commands splendid views of the castle, and the castle commands splendid views right back at it, because they face each other across the park's dead-straight Long Walk, so called because, at 2.65 miles (4.26 km) from one end to the other, it can feel like a bit of a trek.

Royal Ascot and Royal Windsor Racecourses

You may not be surprised to learn that the Royal Ascot and Royal Windsor racecourses both sit within the Crown Estate here – after all, horse racing has long been known as the Sport of Kings and there was another clue in the modifier attached to the otherwise geographical names of the courses. I should think the rates that these two tenants have to pay the Queen are quite high, but I am also fairly confident that they can afford them.

The world-famous Royal Meeting held at Ascot in June each year is important for the running of the Gold Cup. It is also for many the highlight of the social season, not least on Ladies' Day, when ladies get to dress even more as ladies than they do on the other four days of the meeting, when they already dress quite a lot as ladies anyway. We have to come back in July, though, for Ascot's most prestigious race, the King George VI and Queen Elizabeth Stakes: with a prize fund of more than £1 million, it is second only to the Epsom Derby in that respect.

Eton

Pop across the pedestrian Windsor Bridge to the other side of the Thames to find the quaint town of Eton and the fine buildings of its famous college, responsible for producing many British prime ministers and a few foreign despots besides. If you stop off for afternoon tea you should try a traditional Eton mess if it's on the menu, given that it originated in the college in the nineteenth century.

Legoland Windsor

Perhaps surprisingly for a Windsor attraction, Legoland does not belong to the Queen. It didn't always belong to Legoland either; it used to be Windsor Safari Park, until that attraction fell on hard times and had to find alternative homes for all its 600 animals and sea creatures (I understand that Longleat Safari Park did rather well out of it, but they couldn't take the dolphins, which had to go to the Netherlands instead). In any event, Legoland is now a hugely popular mixture of Lego-themed models, rides and building workshops. They even have life-sized models of some animals you might see on safari, which I for one find rather poignant.

Buckinghamshire (J15–J16)

> **❝** To drive on the inside lane of a
> motorway is to advertise your senility
> and your advancing years.
> Not even lorries will go in it. **❞**

Jeremy Clarkson on the addition of a fourth lane
on the M25 between J15 and J16

The M25 doesn't spend too long in Buckinghamshire
and it sticks to the geographically vertical Colne
Valley for the duration. For a long time this valley has
been an obvious natural path for nature and mankind
to use for travelling north or south, and it was also an
opportunity the M25 couldn't afford to miss, which is
why the motorway runs parallel with the Colne River,
the Grand Union Canal and the boundary between
Greater London to the east and Buckinghamshire to
the west.

THE FUNCTIONS OF THE JUNCTIONS

Junction 15 – Colnbrook Interchange

Maltese cross

This junction is the second of our three four-level stacks on the M25, following the one at J7 (the M23 interchange). There are only one or two others in the whole of Britain, and there are three good reasons for their rarity in this country:

→ They are only really needed where traffic flows are immense.

→ They cost about as much as a flight to Mars.

→ If you're not careful, they end up looking like huge, concrete monsters in the sky.

For that latter reason, it is best to disguise them within the natural contours of a rolling landscape, but the terrain around this junction was flat. Undeterred, the M25 designers and builders created their own rolling landscape at the same time constructing 11 bridges and three viaducts up to a height of 69 feet (21 metres). It sounds messy, but if you check out an aerial view of this interchange you will see why it is known in the trade as a 'Maltese cross'. If you can't see it at first, focus on the shape of the slip roads as they curve away from the centre with perfect symmetry. Now you're excited, right? You will also see 'from the air' just how many trees were planted in order to make you feel that you are driving through a beautiful forest as you navigate this junction. If you get stuck in slow-moving traffic here (it does happen, apparently), spend some time admiring the symmetry of the woodland you are passing through. Breathe in through your nose, and out through your mouth. Count slowly to ten and then even more slowly back to one again. When you get home, your family will marvel at how relaxed you seem given that you were recently stuck in a huge tailback on the M25. You're welcome.

The reason that a Maltese cross was required here in the first place, of course, was the need to service Terminals 1, 2 and 3 at Heathrow while still allowing the free passage of the M4 to the west of England and on into Wales. In the other direction, the M4 is also the main artery into the West End of London. The junction takes its name from the brook that runs alongside the Old Slade Reservoir lying below the slip road to the M4 west.

London Heathrow Airport

You've probably heard of Heathrow. It spreads itself across almost 5 square miles (12 square kilometres) and has six terminals, including the cargo one. As the largest operator by far, British Airways has commandeered Terminal 5, but in total around 80 airlines fly to over 80 countries worldwide.

In terms of passengers, Heathrow is the busiest in Europe and the third busiest in the world (after Atlanta and Beijing). Handling over 70 million passengers a year, the most popular international destinations flown to in 2014 were New York (JFK), Dubai and Dublin (in that order). The most popular domestic destination was again Edinburgh.

With an average of 200,000 passengers and 70,000 employees needing to get to and from the airport each day, it's not surprising that the M25 gets a bit busy around these parts.

Junction 16 – Denham Interchange

A bit of a facelift

The junction takes its name from the town of Denham to the east, home to Denham Country Park and the Buckinghamshire Golf Club.

This interchange has but two levels, a mere bagatelle compared to the four-level stack of J15, but it was in fact another complex engineering challenge requiring the removal of much earth and the planting of nearly 200,000 trees in order to provide access to and from the M40 without defacing the appearance of the Alder Bourne Valley within the Colne Valley Park below. It was probably worth the trouble, though, as the M40 takes us north-west up through Buckinghamshire to the Shakespeare country of Warwickshire and on to the Midlands just below Birmingham. In the other direction, it takes us down towards Wembley, home of English football and host to many a music concert (see 'Places to Visit' below).

ON THE ROAD (J15–J16)

Back on the road, as we progress northwards through Buckinghamshire towards Hertfordshire, we remain well and truly in Heathrow territory. We only have to look up at the constant stream of airborne beasts of burden to know that we are passing under the flight path of one of the world's busiest airports. Some of the planes seem so huge from directly below that they appear to be hardly moving, especially the ones that seem to struggle with their full load of fuel as they bank slowly on take-off in order to point in the direction of the bit of the world they might be heading for (which, in the case of Heathrow, could be any bit of the world at all).

The road approaching J15 has two six-lane carriageways, the widest stretch of motorway in the country, and yet it still gets jam-packed. We motorists, of course, blame Highways England for this, in spite of the fact they have given us 12 lanes and a Maltese cross intersection at J15. One day it might occur to us that we are the problem, but then again it probably won't.

Great Western Railway

The railway line that runs east–west below us just after J15 was originally built by engineering genius Isambard Kingdom Brunel as part of the Great Western Railway that opened up Wales and the West Country to the Londoners of the mid nineteenth century. It is currently undergoing a twenty-first-century makeover as part of the east–west Crossrail project that by 2019 will have delivered 62 miles (100 km) of modern railway across London from Reading in the west to Abbey Wood in the east.

Pinewood Studios

The bridge overhead just before J16 leads west to Pinewood Studios, the second of the three film studios we pass by on our tour round the motorway. Like the Shepperton Studios we passed not so long ago, hundreds of classic films have been made here, but the studios are perhaps best known for the bawdy *Carry On* films made between 1958 and 1992 and the James Bond films that began with *Dr No* in 1962 with Sean Connery in the role that every actor wants, and which continue to this day with Daniel Craig as 007. If you do see an Aston Martin DB5 passing you around here, don't mess with it.

The iconic 007 stage at Pinewood Studios is loaned out to other productions in between Bond films and is so large that it housed the entire Greek fishing village featured in the 2008 romcom musical blockbuster *Mamma Mia!* Perhaps the reason that film gave a part to ex-007 Pierce Brosnan was because he had developed squatter's rights on the stage – it certainly wasn't because he could sing.

Just after J16 we will drive under the Oxford Road, part of the A40 trunk road that runs all the way from London to Fishguard on the south-west coast of Wales, and immediately afterwards we will continue downhill to pass under the splendid Chalfont Viaduct.

Chalfont Viaduct

This five-arch, brick railway viaduct was built in 1906 as part of the line to carry trains between London and High Wycombe. Today it forms part of the Chiltern Main Line that runs between London Marylebone and Birmingham.

Before the M25 came along, the River Misbourne ran through the central arch of the bridge, which was awkward, so engineers rerouted the river through a tunnel below the right-hand arch (as we look at it travelling clockwise) and replaced it with the anticlockwise carriageway of the motorway. You have to admire the future-proofing of these Edwardian architects, who allowed just enough width beneath each arch to fit in three lanes of any motorway that might just be built within the next 80 years.

The viaduct gained a certain infamy in recent times with its GIVE PEAS A CHANCE graffiti running along the top on the clockwise side. Apparently, this started life as simply PEAS, the signature of a graffiti artist. Following his continual arrests for property defacement, some other 'artists' thought it would be amusing to supplement his 'signature' to read like a John Lennon spelling mistake or a cry for the vegetarians of the world to unite in the ongoing struggle against meat-eating.

PLACES TO VISIT (J15–J16)

Royal Botanic Gardens, Kew

At J15 head east on the M4 towards London to find Kew Gardens not far from where the M4 comes to its natural end. The biggest collection of living plants on earth is found here, spread across a vast, beautifully landscaped area containing an arboretum, a waterlily house, a treetop walkway, an aquatic garden, an alpine house, a Chinese pagoda, a conservatory with ten different climatic zones, and of course the world-famous palm house, a cathedral-like structure that draws us in to worship the many plants it holds. It comes as no great surprise to learn that UNESCO designated the attraction a World Heritage Site in 2003.

Colne Valley Park

This vast park is the first real countryside we come to west of London, and it never disappoints. It runs from the Thames in the south (just to the west of Heathrow) to the lakes of Rickmansworth in the north, incorporating numerous country parks and nature reserves as it goes, and playing genial host to the Colne River and the Grand Union Canal, Britain's most important inland waterway. Pretty much any junction from 13 to 17 will allow us to access the park at some point or other, but the lovely village of Denham off J16 (via the M40 in the direction of London) is particularly good for accessing the river and canal.

The park's 43 square miles (111 square kilometres) of landscape include wetlands, woodlands, chalk valleys and flat plains, and the list of things to do here is accordingly a long one: walking, cycling, horseriding, golf, birdwatching, wildlife-spotting, narrowboating, sailing, canoeing, angling, windsurfing and water skiing. I think I need to go and lie down.

Wembley

From J16 follow the brown tourist signs for New Wembley Stadium, which lies south-east towards London. The huge football stadium was opened in 2007 to replace the old stadium that had been demolished four years earlier and, as we have seen, recycled materials arising from that demolition were used in 2005 to widen the M25 between J12 and J15.

With 90,000 seats, the bowl-shaped stadium is the second largest in Europe. It is also the most user-friendly stadium known to man, because its 2,618 toilets are more than we will find at any other venue in the world. Its iconic arch, which can be seen for miles around, may look quite slender from a distance but its interior is in fact big enough to run a train through from one end to the other.

The stadium is most famous, of course, for hosting the FA Cup Final every year, as well as being the venue at which the English national side play their home matches, but nowadays it hosts a number of other finals and play-off matches, plus a rugby league final and some American football games, so there's no excuse for not going.

If you prefer music to sport (although the stadium does sometimes host music concerts as well), you don't have to go far from here to find the indoor Wembley Arena, which has been putting on the world's top acts for decades. From the Beatles to Iron Maiden, from Cliff Richard to Fall Out Boy, no genre has been left unturned.

> **❝***I've fond memories of the time it was the venue for large-scale ecstasy deals and the rendezvous for ravers. Excellent Harvester as well…***❞**

Will Self on South Mimms Services

We will have passed into Hertfordshire not long after J16 and our trip through the county will see us intersect with Britain's first complete motorway and enjoy a literal watershed. We will marvel at yet more engineering achievements and assess what makes South Mimms service station both famous and infamous. We will finish by travelling back to the future, having made the most of our second opportunity to ignore the United Nations.

THE FUNCTIONS OF THE JUNCTIONS

Junction 17 – Maple Cross Interchange

Last stop for the Colne Valley Park

A minor junction that exists to serve local communities like the eponymous Maple Cross and Heronsgate but, unless you live hereabouts, it's probably more useful as a setting-off point for the northern end of the Colne Valley Park, including the Stocker's Lake Nature Reserve and the Batchworth Lock Canal Centre.

Junction 18 – Chorleywood Interchange

Underground, overground

This is the interchange with the A404 trunk road that runs from Paddington to serve the north-west of London before flying over the M25 on its way into Buckinghamshire. The A404 runs largely parallel here with London Undergound's Metropolitan Line on its way to Amersham, which is the railway line we just drove over as we approached this junction. The interchange takes its name from the nearby village of Chorleywood and its fine common, which sits within the Chilterns Area of Outstanding Natural Beauty.

Junction 19 – Chandler's Cross Interchange

The introvert

J19 only has eyes for the inside of the M25 and doesn't even bother to offer a slip road that would take us west to the outside world. It heads straight east to the Watford Road, thereby focussing its efforts on serving the community that gives that fine road its name. Given that Watford is the largest single settlement within the M25 perimeter, this does seem to make some sense. It does make one exception to its rule about only serving Watford, though, as its brown tourist signs will whisk us off in no time at all to the nearby Warner Bros Studio Tour, which, as we will see in 'Places to Visit', is really just the Harry Potter Studio Tour for the time being. The people responsible for naming motorway junctions have once more betrayed their lack of imagination here, plumping for the nearby settlement of Chandler's Cross and sticking Interchange on the end.

Junction 20 – Hunton Bridge Interchange
The versatile A41

Another junction named after a nearby settlement, the primary job of this one is to feed to and from the A41. If we head south-east towards Central London on this trunk road, we will ultimately be rewarded for our efforts with a whole host of attractions, including Abbey Road Studios and *that* zebra crossing, Lord's Cricket Ground, Regent's Park and its zoo, the Sherlock Holmes Museum and Madame Tussauds on Baker Street.

The A41 also does a splendid job heading north-west. It soon feeds off to Hemel Hempstead, one of the new towns built after the Second World War to house Londoners displaced by the Blitz, and then carries on up to Aylesbury, the county town of Buckinghamshire.

Junction 21/21A – Chiswell Interchange
Double trouble (2)

The powers that name junctions nearly called this one after nearby Chiswell Green, but couldn't quite be bothered in the end. Nevertheless, this all-important link with the M1 is the third of our three four-level stacks on the M25; it required such a complex engineering solution that the powers that allocate junction numbers decided to number it J21 *and* J21A just to make sure we got the message. The double-junction system was considered necessary to cope with the heavy traffic that passes through here in all directions and resulted in J21 being appointed to carry traffic to and from the northbound M1 only and J21A being dedicated to carry traffic to and from the southbound M1 only. J21 is further complicated by having the clockwise slip road pass over the M1 and the anticlockwise slip road pass under the M1. I am pleased to have made all that clear for you.

I also hope and pray that the engineering genius that was employed to make this interchange work is not lost on you just because they planted 130,000 trees and shrubs to leave the area looking like they'd never even been near the place with as much as a single bulldozer.

The point of all this effort, of course, was to allow free and easy access to Britain's first complete motorway, the M1 that runs for 193.5 miles (311.4 km) to link London with Leeds and York in the north and serves a host of other major towns and cities along the way. One other benefit much nearer to the M25 itself is the access this junction affords to London Luton Airport to the north.

London Luton Airport

I know what many of you are thinking. If the distance from London to Luton is 33.9 miles (54.6 km), how can Luton be in London? It isn't, of course, but every major city in the world is now up to that old trick for marketing purposes.

In its defence, though, London Luton Airport is less than 30 minutes by train to the capital, and only 15 minutes by car on a good day to the M25, which is quite near London really. What's more, as we shall see in the Essex chapter, London Stansted Airport and (wait for it!) London Southend Airport are even further from Central London than London Luton Airport is, so there!

The airport is best known for being home to low-cost carriers EasyJet, Monarch, Thomson Airways and Ryanair, all of whom have bases at Luton. Most flights go to destinations within Europe, the most popular in 2014 being Budapest followed by Amsterdam and Bucharest. Glasgow was the most popular domestic destination.

European Route 13

You probably think of J21/J21A on the M25 as the interchange with the M1, unless of course you work for the United Nations Economic Commission for Europe, in which case you probably know it as the interchange with European Route E13 at the point it intersects with European Route E30 (which we will come to shortly).

Unlike most of its International E-road Network, though, the UN didn't bother to join lots of roads it has nothing to do with in lots of different countries to make the E13. It didn't even bother to join lots of roads it has nothing to do with in Britain. It just looked at the M1 and decided to designate most of it the E13. If that all sounds a little parochial to you, I would like to point out that the clever people who dream up these ideas in Geneva have in many other cases expanded their horizons beyond belief. They have, for example, decided that Europe, for the purposes of encouraging trade within its member states, includes Canada, the USA, Central Asia and Israel. I think they were struggling to spend their annual US$50 million budget before extending Europe to ensure that demand for their schemes could finally keep up with supply.

Junction 22 – The Bell Roundabout

Watershed moment

When I say that J22 is something of a watershed, I mean that J22 is something of a watershed. Literally. If rain falls to the west of J22, it runs towards the River Colne and on down to the Thames not far from J13 (Runnymede). If rain falls to the east of J22, it will run towards the Lea Navigation between J25 (Waltham Cross) and J26 (Waltham Abbey) and then down to the Thames near Canary Wharf to the east of London.

The junction itself serves the city of St Albans to the north and a number of local communities such as London Colney and Shenley. Shenley was famous for many years in the last century for its groundbreaking mental health hospital, although it would have started life in the 1930s as a 'lunatic asylum'. Like so many others of its kind, it was previously a country house on a large estate (as homes to the landed gentry, many of them had a long, curved drive to ensure privacy from the road, which is how the term 'going round the bend' originated).

Arsenal and Watford football clubs have their training grounds just off this junction on the south side. Arsenal's state-of-the-art facility was opened in 2000, whereupon Watford snapped up the offer of their old one next door.

The junction is named after The Bell Roundabout that already existed when the motorway came along and commandeered it. The Bell Roundabout was named after The Bell public house that sat alongside it. The Bell public house, I am devastated to have to tell you, is now a McDonald's. Let's not bother updating the name of the junction, eh?

Junction 23 – Bignell's Corner

Cutbush city limit

One of the largest roundabouts in the UK, this junction is built over three levels in order to link the M25 to the A1(M), at the point where the A1 north from London becomes motorway. It is named after a garden centre (Bignell and Cutbush) that used to sit here, but is unofficially known as the South Mimms junction on account of the services that exist at the top of the roundabout on the north side of the motorway.

The A1 south from here will take us down past Arsenal's Emirates Stadium and on through Islington all the way down to St Paul's Cathedral. Taking the A1(M) north from here, and using it in conjunction with the stretches of the A1 it hasn't yet replaced, will take us to Edinburgh if we stick at it long enough.

Junction 24 – Potters Bar Interchange

Does what it says on the tin

A minor junction that exists only to serve the surrounding area; in particular, the town of Potters Bar to the north.

Junction 25 – Waltham Cross Interchange

London Bridge to King's Lynn trunk road

This junction links primarily to the A10, a major trunk road that runs from London Bridge all the way up to King's Lynn and the nearby royal estate of Sandringham on the north Norfolk coast. Nearer to home the junction serves Enfield Town (which has the unusual claim to fame of having hosted the world's first cash machine in 1967) to the south and Hertford, the county town of (you guessed it) Hertfordshire to the north. Even nearer to home, as the junction name suggests, it has the great pleasure of serving Waltham Cross (more of which in 'Places to Visit' below).

ON THE ROAD (J17–J25)

Now we know what the Hertfordshire junctions are for, we can rewind to drive the width of the county. The motorway has brought us up and round from Buckinghamshire and will take us on into Essex in the east, but in the meantime we will enjoy some very nice views, a few impressive buildings, a fine canal setting (if we're quick) and any number of red kites. Once we get clear of J20, we are going to be able to see a lot more of our surroundings as we travel along the northern section of the orbit, for the conscientious objectors of the north proved to be less objectionable than their fellow objectors in the south (although there are a couple of notable exceptions to this rule, as we shall see).

Let's Go Fly a Kite

Now that the Heathrow planes have largely disappeared from view, we will see in their place the growing numbers of red kite that now inhabit the skies between J16 and J21, circling and hovering until a dinner of carrion is once more served up by a passing motorist.

We will look at the remarkable comeback of the red kite from near extinction in the chapter headed 'The Natural World of the M25'.

Church versus State

Off J20 to the north is Kings Langley, so called because the palace there was home to the Plantagenet Kings of England for 300 years. To the south is Abbotts Langley, the bit of Langley that the church was allowed to keep until it got too big for its boots and messed once too often with Henry VIII. Abbotts Langley had been so powerful at one time that in 1154 one of its sons, Nicholas Breakspear, became the first and only Englishman ever to be elected pope. Sadly, he is best remembered for his cause of death, having choked after swallowing a fly that had been for a swim in his wine glass. There is little friction nowadays between the royal family and the church around these parts, but only because the M25 keeps them apart, another benefit of building motorways that goes largely unsung, I fear.

Cheers to the Gade Valley Viaduct!

The Gade Valley that runs down below J20 has long been a useful natural path between London and those parts of Britain that lie to the north and west. It is the path through which the River Gade runs south from its spring in the Chiltern Hills through Hertfordshire to the Colne Valley. The Gade was the valley of choice for the builders of the Grand Union Canal as they linked the industrial powerhouses of London and Birmingham in the eighteenth century; and it was the obvious best option for the new railways of the nineteenth century to be routed through this area – even today, as part of the West Coast Main Line, it remains a primary rail route all the way to Scotland. Once roads arrived in the twentieth century, the valley was soon playing host to the A41 trunk road linking London to Birkenhead on the Mersey.

The issue for the M25, therefore, was how to cross over all the stuff that was already there; and the Gade Valley Viaduct was the answer. The longest bridge on the motorway (leaving aside the Queen Elizabeth II Bridge, which of course isn't really on the motorway anyway), its double-wine-glass-shaped concrete pillars support eleven 138-foot (42-metre) spans to produce a grand total of 1,516 feet (462 metres) of viaduct. We'll know we're approaching it in spite of the high banks on either side of us because we'll be able to see a view that stretches out a long way in front of us (including the curve of the viaduct itself), and once we are on it we will again hear double thuds as our tyres hit the expansion joints.

All Saints Pastoral Centre

Just before J22 on the north side, there is a fine view to be had of the old All Saints Pastoral Centre, a Victorian building that started life as a convent in 1901 before being converted for use as a pastoral retreat in 1973 and more recently sold off to property developers as a residential plot.

Keep Right on to the End of the Road

At the fourth bridge after J22 we again duck under Watling Street, the Roman road we last encountered between J1a and J1b on its long way from Durovernum Cantiacorum (Canterbury) to Viroconium Cornoviorum (Wroxeter in Shropshire). This time it crosses over as the A5, having run here in a pretty straight line all the way from the start of the Edgware Road at Marble Arch right bang in the centre of London. It has been afforded another dull concrete flyover here, hardly befitting its status and proof once more that road builders have little respect for history, but it carries on regardless with the dogged determination that characterised the empire that first built it.

South Mimms Services

Out of the frying pan and into the fire

Sitting just north of the roundabout at J23, the Welcome Break Services here were originally opened in 1987, but were destroyed by a fire caused by an unattended frying pan in Julie's Pantry in 1998. Temporary huts and vans continued to provide much-needed relief to drivers until a rebuilt service station finally opened in late 1999. That hangar-style building today reflects the changing nature of the nation's eating habits as more and more healthier-food outlets stand alongside the more traditional cholesterol-ridden ones. South Mimms is also unusual in being the only services in Britain linked to the National Cycle Network (on Route 12, known as the Great North Way).

Becoming famous

South Mimms became proper cool in May 1998 when Robbie Williams turned up to sing his part for the video of the England World Cup Song ('Three Lions') that year. The services also appeared on Sky TV's *Brainiac: Science Abuse* 'edutainment' programme in 2006 and on the BBC's *EastEnders* soap opera in 2012.

There is even an entire book devoted to the service station. Written in 2004 by Roger Green, based on his week-long stay there, his observations are entitled *Destination Nowhere: A South Mimms Motorway Service Station Diary*. In 2007 the services were also the subject of Luke Wright's poem 'It's Mimms O'Clock', describing the sanctuary that the pit stop provides for weary travellers, especially those with irritable children in tow – it was one of ten poems written about the M25 at the time by poetry collective Aisle 16.

Becoming infamous

For many years South Mimms was notorious as a drop-off point for illegal entrants and asylum seekers who had arrived on lorries from the Continent, not least because the immigrants could easily head north from here on the A1(M). Its geographical position certainly affords a quick getaway in pretty much any direction and this also made it popular over the years for a wide variety of criminal activities. Here is but a sample:

➔ **1990**: Police found the mutilated body of a woman who remains unidentified to this day.

→ **2001**: Police seized drugs with a street value of £12 million from an HGV that had been driven up from Spain.

→ **2005**: A Londoner known as the Jihad Plumber was caught in the car park trying to buy weapons including three Uzi sub-machine guns and a rocket launcher.

→ **2013**: 2,900 identical dresses valued at £17,000 in total were stolen from the lorry park.

Queen Wilhelmina of South Mimms

Queen Wilhelmina of the Netherlands fled to South Mimms village (as opposed to South Mimms service station) to escape Nazi occupation and provide much-needed inspiration through her radio broadcasts to the Dutch resistance movement during the Second World War. She narrowly escaped death during a German air attack on the country house she was staying at, but her guards were killed. I assume the Germans were intent on bombing the Queen herself, because I can't think of another reason to bomb poor little South Mimms.

The Old New River

As we start to pass through J25, or as we start to take the slip road off to the A10, an enclosed concrete bridge runs overhead. This was built to allow the New River (which is in fact a centuries-old canal) to cross over the motorway and thereby carry on supplying London with drinking water, a job it has been fulfilling since the early seventeenth century. A long concrete slab with metal railings on either side runs along the top of the aqueduct to allow the water company access at both ends for maintenance purposes. It is also used by walkers enjoying the New River Path, a long-distance footpath that runs 28 miles (45 km) from Hertford to Islington in North London.

Hold That High Street!

In order to appease the restless natives of Waltham Cross east of J25, the Holmesdale Tunnel, along with 4 miles (6.4 km) of embankments and acoustic fences, was built to create a corridor that allows the motorway to pass relatively unobtrusively through the heavily built-up residential and industrial areas around here. Construction of this cut-and-cover tunnel was difficult because it had to be built in a natural trough (drainage, for example, is a bit easier if you're building a tunnel at or near a summit, because gravity will come to your assistance, as was the case with the Bell Common Tunnel that we will come to shortly). The Holmesdale Tunnel was made even more difficult because the engineers had to allow for the busy Waltham Cross

High Street above to be shored up and kept open during construction, and ultimately to be carried over the eastern edge of the tunnel's roof. The rest of the tunnel, once completed, was covered with topsoil to form a park and recreation area.

Back to the Future

Having travelled back in time just after Clacket Lane service station 20 junctions ago (between J5 and J6), we will once more cross the Prime Meridian Line about halfway between J25 and J26, thereby re-entering the Eastern Hemisphere of planet earth. Immediately after we do so we will rather appropriately cross from Hertfordshire into Essex, the county of the East Saxons. If you wanted to avoid the Eastern Hemisphere today, I'm afraid you have now come too far.

Just as on the southern stretch of the M25, no one around here cares whether or not we want to know exactly when we change hemispheres, but at least there are some clues on this occasion. Just after the motorway passes clockwise over the Lea Navigation and the River Lea in quick succession, it passes over the A121, which is called Meridian Way, so I think this is as good a point as any to let out a cheer. If you can't take your eyes off the road to spot the water channels or the road below, simply cheer when you drive between the electricity pylons on either side of the road (they are running along Meridian Way anyway). By way of further confirmation that you have cheered at the right moment, you will now see the Meridian Business

Park on your right, the one which contains the huge Sainsbury's Distribution Centre.

If you remain unsatisfied and really, really want to enjoy a close-up physical manifestation of the Meridian Line, simply pop off at J25 or J26 and head for nearby Waltham Abbey, where the vertical centre of the earth is in fact marked out by a symbolic blue arch within the Abbey Gardens.

PLACES TO VISIT (J17–J25)
Warner Bros Harry Potter Studio Tour

To visit the Warner Bros Studio Tour at Leavesden, follow the brown tourist signs for just 3 miles (4.8 km) from J19. Since this former aerodrome was converted to film studios in the 1990s, notable films to have come off the production line have included the 007 blockbuster *Goldeneye*, the *Star Wars* prequels and the Batman film *The Dark Knight*, but they really hit the big time with *Harry Potter and the Philosopher's Stone* in 2001, the first of eight Harry Potter films that would be made there over a ten-year period. The studio tour is currently given over completely to the Harry Potter sets, where apparently everything feels truly magical except the hole in your wallet, which is said to feel very real indeed. They probably thought that a race known as Muggles would be an easy touch, and so it has proved.

St Albans

Served by J21A and J22, the city and historic market town of St Albans is popular as a commuter town and as a tourist destination. That it was once an important Roman settlement on Watling Street is recognised by the contents of the Verulamium Museum and in the naming of Verulamium Park. Today its main attractions include its fifteenth-century clock tower, marketplace, Roman ruins, Anglo-Saxon church and Ye Olde Fighting Cocks pub (one of the oldest in England). Topping even that illustrious bill, though, is St Albans Cathedral, which started life as a Benedictine abbey (the gateway of which still stands) before being revamped by the Normans and then promoted to cathedral status in 1877. It is the second-longest cathedral in England after Chichester but has the longest nave. St Albans 1 Chichester 1.

Hatfield House

Not far north on the A1(M) off J23 we will come to Hatfield House, home to the Marquess and Marchioness of Salisbury, and once owned by Henry VIII to house his offspring. Those children, of course, went on to become Edward VI, Mary I and Elizabeth I, the latter learning that she was to become Queen of England at this very house. I'm not sure how much time they spent here together, but perhaps the reason Edward was always such a sickly child was because he had to play at Hatfield with Bloody Mary and the future nemesis of the mighty Spanish Armada?

A visit to the house will reward us with views of fine paintings and tapestries, grand staircases and stained-glass windows, not to mention the sublime gardens and the fine Jacobean house itself, which have been the setting of many a TV programme and film. When Angelina Jolie was filmed playing action-girl Lara Croft here, Mary and Elizabeth would probably have loved it, while Edward would probably have hidden himself behind a tapestry – perhaps the one with the unicorn on it, for extra protection.

Trotters Bottom

Trotters Bottom is a short country road running along the edge of a golf course just south of J23. Nothing ever happens there. I just wanted to write Trotters Bottom (three times).

Waltham Cross

Just north of J25, sitting in the very south-east corner of Hertfordshire, on the border with Essex to the east and Greater London to the south, Waltham Cross has a number of claims to fame, including the following:

→ At its centre stands one of the three surviving (but much restored) Eleanor Crosses erected in the late thirteenth century by Edward I, as we have already seen, to commemorate the overnight stops of his beloved Queen Eleanor of Castile, on her funeral procession south to the capital. Without the Eleanor Cross, Waltham Cross would be plain old Waltham.

→ The Lee Valley White Water Centre, which adjoins the River Lee Navigation to the east of the town, hosted the canoe slalom event in the London 2012 Olympics.

→ Waltham Cross is the only town outside Greater London to be served by a Transport for London night bus, the N279.

Paradise Wildlife Park

J25 is another junction popular with children because its brown tourist signs lead to this popular attraction in Broxbourne, home to over 400 animals ranging from farmyard animals to big cats, and from Burmese pythons to marmosets. Children are allowed to feed and touch many of the animals, something I would be quite excited about if I were a Burmese python.

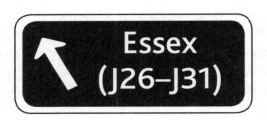

**Essex
(J26–J31)**

The views to the right of the motorway between J26 and J27 are of Epping Forest, whose northern edge we will skirt until we reach the Bell Common Tunnel, which takes us right underneath it. Once clear of the forest, we take the wide right-hand sweep down through the surprisingly undulating hills of Essex before we reach the flatter marshes of that same county in order to get back to where we started on the Thames Estuary at the Dartford Crossing. Nothing much is hidden from our view on this final stretch of the journey, as we cut through the renegade North Ockendon, enjoy a final cup of tea together at Thurrock Services, and skip four weddings to go straight to a funeral.

THE FUNCTIONS OF THE JUNCTIONS

Junction 26 – Waltham Abbey Interchange

Recreational gateway

It goes without saying that the Waltham Abbey Interchange is pretty handy for Waltham Abbey, but it may be less obvious that it is also the gateway to the huge Lee Valley Regional Park and the ancient woodland of Epping Forest (see 'Places to Visit' below for more information about all three destinations).

Junction 27 – Theydon Bois Interchange
Seven bridges
Named after the nearby settlement that has bagged a few Best Kept Village awards in its time (more of which in 'Places to Visit' below), this junction's sole purpose is nonetheless to interchange with the north–south M11. In order to keep construction down to two levels to minimise the impact on the surrounding valley, seven bridges were required, including five that had to be built over the live M11 at the time.

The M11 north will take us to Stansted Airport en route to the university town of Cambridge. The M11 south will take us down through the suburbs of north-east London.

London Stansted Airport

I know what many of you are thinking again. If London Stansted is 38.7 miles (62 km) from Central London, surely that means it's not in London? Well, ditto what I said about London Luton, even if London Stansted is 5 miles (8 km) further out than London Luton from

Central London and a further 10 minutes out from the M25.

The airport is best known as the main base for low-cost carrier Ryanair, which flies to over 100 destinations from here, but Stansted is in reality far more versatile than that. At the other end of the price scale, another airline to have a strong base here is Harrods Aviation, which handles private jets for the rich and famous, as well as taking care of state visits and having its own small helicopter fleet. If you have to ask how much it costs to fly on one of the two Air Harrods helicopters, you can't afford it. The Ryanair check-in desk is over in the main terminal, so off you go.

The most popular destination for standard humans from Stansted is Dublin, followed by Rome-Ciampino and Bergamo, with Edinburgh the most popular domestic destination.

European Route E30

We have seen how the UN-designated Route E15 parasites itself onto the M25 between J24 and J1b, including therefore the entire Dartford Crossing, as part of its north–south journey from Inverness to the Bay of Gibraltar, and how it has 'borrowed' the M1 as its very own E13.

The United Nations has also seen fit to borrow the M25 between J15 (M4 interchange) and J27 (M11 interchange) for its west–east E30 route, which runs 3,760 miles (6,050 km) from Cork in Ireland to Omsk in Russia, via Moscow and including a long stretch through Siberia.

This means that the UN manages to leech itself onto the M25 twice on the same stretch between J24 (Potters Bar) and J27 (M11 interchange), as both the E15 and the E30. The next time you are driving on this stretch of the motorway, be very careful not to leave at J27 in the direction of Moscow if it is in fact your intention to head south for the Bay of Gibraltar from J1b, an all too easy mistake to make if you're as confused as the people who devised the United Nations International E-road Network (which, to be fair, you're probably not).

Junction 28 – Brook Street Interchange

The Canary Wharf to Great Yarmouth trunk road

Named after a nearby residential suburb of Brentwood, this three-level intersection (with a roundabout as the middle level) exists to feed to and from the A12, which runs 129 miles (208 km) north-east from London to the Norfolk Broads.

Heading south-west from J28, the A12 will take us down past the Queen Elizabeth Olympic Park in Stratford to the Blackwall Tunnel beside Canary Wharf in east London. Heading north-east from J28 it will take us up through Essex and Suffolk until we finally reach the coastal resort of Great Yarmouth in Norfolk.

The railway that runs over the motorway just after J28 carries the mainline London Liverpool Street to Norwich service.

Junction 29 – Cranham Interchange

Southend Arterial Road

This junction takes its name from a residential suburb to the south-west, but is also known as Codham Hall Interchange after an agricultural/equestrian area to the east. It serves the east–west A127, known as the Southend Arterial Road.

We can take the A127 a short way west to join the A12 at Gallows Corner, so called because the crossroads there used to be so popular with highwaymen intent on holding up stagecoaches that it was worth the while of the authorities to erect a gallows on the spot. This saved transporting the highway robbers elsewhere to be strung up – an immediate suspended sentence that saved suspending the sentence, if you will.

Alternatively, we can take the A127 a much longer way east to Southend-on-Sea, the playground of the tangoed nouveau riche of Essex, where Estuary English is positively de rigueur. Southend Pier is the longest pleasure pier in the world, so if you like your pleasure long and bracing, this is the pier for you. The other reason for heading out this way, of course, is to get to London Southend Airport.

London Southend Airport

Of the six airports that claim to be in London, London Southend takes the long-distance biscuit at 41.8 miles (67.3 km) from the equestrian statue of King Charles I at the top of Whitehall (the point from which, you may remember, all distances from London are measured).

Over a million passengers now travel from here each year, primarily (in 2014) to Amsterdam, followed by Alicante and Barcelona, but none have been more famous than the one who in 1963 drove his Aston Martin DB5 straight onto a transport plane bound for Geneva. That man was, of course, Sean Connery, determined (as secret agent 007) to track down the villainous Auric Goldfinger.

Junction 30 – Mar Dyke Interchange

Thames Gateway

This interchange is built over the eponymous Mar Dyke river ditch that we can see flowing underneath us on either side of the road on the south side of the junction, and it exists primarily to serve the A13, yet another main artery in and out of London.

The A13 west (known in part as the Thames Gateway) runs parallel with the Thames to take us in past Dagenham, London City Airport and the financial district of Canary Wharf before reaching its conclusion in Commercial Road in London's East End. Dagenham, of course, is home to the famous Ford motor plant that re-entered public consciousness in recent times after the release of the 2010 film *Made in Dagenham* about the female sewing machinists' strike there in 1968.

The A13 east runs parallel with the A127 to the north to eventually deposit us in the same place, Southend. Along the way we skirt the northern edge of Hadleigh Country Park.

J30 is also the main exit for Lakeside Shopping Centre and Thurrock Services, both of which we shall return to shortly.

Even if we don't want to exit the motorway at J30, we can't help doing so of course, because this is the point at which the road itself stops being the M25 to become the 50-mph (80-km/h) A282 until we are safely across the Thames, and it is for that same reason that the road signs suddenly become green as opposed to motorway blue.

London City Airport

Finally, a London airport that is within touching distance of London! The airport lies about 16 miles (26 km) west along the A13 from J30, so I reckon (taking account of the fast through-airport times at London City Airport) that you could be in Nice within 4 hours of exiting at this junction. Go for it!

Junction 31 – Purfleet Interchange

Junction 30's little helper

In addition to helping J30 deliver motorists to Thurrock Services and Lakeside Shopping Centre, J31 serves local communities such as Purfleet and West Thurrock. It also provides one last chance to get off the road before having to pay the charge to cross the Queen Elizabeth II Bridge.

ON THE ROAD (J26–J31)

Now we know what the Essex junctions are for, let's go back to the point at which Hertfordshire handed over the baton and drive the remainder of the orbit to get us back to where we started at the Dartford Crossing.

Guess the Number of Baked Beans

The Sainsbury's distribution warehouse between J25 and J26 on the south side of the motorway (the one we noted just after crossing the Meridian Line near Waltham Abbey) is truly monstrous. I don't know if you can get your head round 750,000 square feet or 70,000 square metres or 23,000 pallets, but we're talking about a lot of tins, packets and boxes. Just how many baked beans do you think there might be in there? There are over 4 miles (7 km) of conveyor belts to move stuff in and around and out of the centre. If you see a lot of Sainsbury's lorries along this stretch of the M25, you shouldn't be surprised.

Copped Hall

As the road climbs up Epping Forest between J26 and J27 we are afforded occasional views of Copped Hall on the left side, although the views are undoubtedly better travelling anticlockwise. This once great hall is under restoration, having played host in its glorious past to Tudor Queens Mary I and Elizabeth I. Whilst exiled there in 1551, Mary I (when she was still Princess Mary) caused a bit of a stir by taking Catholic Mass in the house, whereas Elizabeth I, a much cheerier sort altogether, is said to have attended the very first performance of *A Midsummer Night's Dream* there.

M25 Stops Play

The Bell Common Tunnel between J26 and J27 was extended from the 200 metres originally proposed by the Department for Transport to its current length of 450 metres in order to better protect the northern tip of Epping Forest above, and in particular to protect the deer, badgers and cricketers who inhabit that space. During the two years it took to construct the curved cut-and-cover tunnel the Epping Foresters Cricket Club agreed to play as a wandering club on the understanding that their pitch and pavilion would be reinstated on the same common land above the tunnel once its cutting had been covered over, and that duly happened. Should you find yourself delayed within the tunnel or on its approaches, you should put this down to slow play and accept the fact with the same degree of stoicism that you would employ were you seated in the pavilion above watching a Herts and Essex Cricket League match. It is the English way, after all.

The Well-guarded Junction 27

After the Bell Common Tunnel comes the descent to J27 (the M11 interchange), with fine views all around. Standing guard on the hill to the right just after the junction is All Saints Church in Theydon Garnon, and standing guard on the hill to the left shortly after that is Hill Hall, the magnificent Elizabethan mansion now run by English Heritage.

Old McDonald Had a Farm

Appearing on the left not long before J28 will be the Old McDonald's Farm family attraction, so expect the kids to scream and scream until you agree to go there and let them enjoy Bouncy Barn, Rubber Duck Race, Battle Barn, Remote Control Tractors, the petting farm and dozens of other attractions that will keep them hyper for hours. At least they might sleep for the rest of the journey home if you succumb.

If you really don't have time to indulge them, they will in any event be able to see the llamas that drew the short straw when it came to deciding which animals should get the enclosure nearest to the M25.

Nearly There!

From about 9 miles out, just after J29, we start to see the supports of the Queen Elizabeth II Bridge and therefore the point at which we started the orbital journey we are on. The supports will loom ever larger as we approach our finish line, but never quite as large, of course, as the even taller chimney of the Littlebrook Power Station on the far side of the river.

Thurrock Services

Situated between J30 and J31, and accessible from both, these Moto services claimed to be the most advanced in the world when they opened in the early nineties. I suspect they're not claiming that now, and it was never going to be easy living next door to the giant

Lakeside Shopping Centre, but they do still provide the usual relief and sustenance to any weary travellers who don't have time to pop next door.

When Lord Adonis paid one of his surprise visits as Secretary of State for Transport in 2009, his main comment was that the services had been greatly improved by the arrival of Marks & Spencer. Coming from a Labour Party politician, albeit one with a name more suited to the Whig or Tory Parties of the eighteenth century, this was a hell of an admission.

The Need for Speed

If we have been moving a bit slowly on the M25 and want to remember what speed looks like just before driving up onto the Queen Elizabeth II Bridge, we can look down at the High Speed 1 Rail Link running below the approach road we are on, yet above the exit lanes from the Dartford Tunnels below to our right. In other words, the High Speed 1 line slices through the air above the tunnel exits but below the bridge approach.

Since 2007 it has been possible to see Eurostar trains speeding to and from the Continent at up to 143 mph (230 km/h) here – the trains are capable of 186 mph (300 km/h) but are only allowed to reach those speeds east of Ebbsfleet in Kent. They have their own tunnel under the Thames just to the east of the bridge (on our left) and any eastbound trains bound for the Continent will slither in there about two seconds after we see them rushing past underneath us (while any St Pancras-bound trains heading west, of course, will just have slithered out of there at the same speed).

We Have Looped the Loop!

As we rise up to the bridge, we are finally back where our circumnavigation began 33 junctions, six counties and 117 miles (188 km) ago. Driving at a steady 70 mph (113 km/h) and without braking, it would have taken us about 1 hour 40 minutes to complete one such lap of the motorway. If you want to have a go at proving this, I suggest setting out about 2 a.m., which gives you the added advantage of not having to pay any charge at the Dartford Crossing.

PLACES TO VISIT (J26–J31)

A famous abbey, a Donkey Derby, acres and acres of outdoor recreational opportunities, a large helping of nature and some iconic film locations make it worth our while popping off at a few of the junctions around Essex.

Lee Valley Regional Park

Follow the brown tourist signs from J25 or J26 to access this huge recreational area. It stretches north–south for 26 miles (42 km) from Ware in Hertfordshire down through Essex and Greater London to the Thames at London's East India Docks. At four times the size of the much more famous Richmond Park in south-west London, it is 10,000 acres (40 square kilometres) of rivers, canals, streams, marinas, marshes, reservoirs, urban green spaces, nature reserves, country parks, golf courses and sports centres. There is quite a lot to do in it!

It got itself seriously promoted in time for the London 2012 Olympic and Paralympic Games, as its southern half was extended and developed to form the Olympic Park itself. The Lee Valley Regional Park Authority still runs three Olympic legacy venues today: the Lee Valley VeloPark (known affectionately as the Pringle during the Olympics), the Lee Valley Hockey and Tennis Centre (formerly known as Eton Manor) and the Lee Valley White Water Centre.

The closest part of the regional park to the M25 here is the River Lee Country Park to the north, sharing itself between Essex and Hertfordshire on either side as it runs north to Broxbourne. It comprises 1,000 acres (4 square kilometres) of lakes, watercourses, footpaths, cycle tracks and open spaces, incorporating Waltham Abbey Woods and long stretches of the River Lee and Lee Navigation, including the Lee Valley White Water Centre itself.

Waltham Abbey

As we have already noted, a symbolic blue arch within the gardens of Waltham Abbey marks out the vertical centre of the earth, the Meridian Line. Another reason to pop off at J26 to visit the abbey is that the churchyard contains the tombstone of King Harold II, runner-up at the Battle of Hastings in 1066. It's not totally certain who it is in the grave below that tombstone, as many different rumours circulated about Harold's mortal remains in the years following his defeat, but it's as good a place as any to go to pay homage to him (unless you're still a bit miffed that he lost the entire country to the French for 400 years and left us saying things like 'let's rendezvous later down the cul-de-sac' – in which case, just leave it).

Epping Forest

J26 is also the ideal stepping stone to Epping Forest. With 6,000 acres (24 square km) of trees, the forest here has long been considered the lungs of London. Although it straddles the border with Essex, it is managed by the City of London for the common good of all who enter. Special events happen throughout the year alongside the more regular activities of walking, horse riding, angling, running, football and golf, while birdwatching, deer-spotting and tree-hugging are also on the Epping Forest menu.

As a former royal hunting forest, it also has some proper history attached to it, including Queen Elizabeth's Hunting Lodge, a white three-storey Tudor timber lodge, which is open to the public. It was erected for Henry VIII and later enjoyed by his daughter Elizabeth I, from where she shot any deer that came too close. In 1882 it was Queen Victoria who gave the land to all the peoples of the land as their natural playground, even turning up in person to open it officially that year.

If You Go Down to the Woods Today...

There is a darker side to Epping Forest, what with tales of witchcraft, ghostly apparitions and human sacrifice in the dead of night, and given its popularity as a burial area for murder victims over the years. Some of the bodies discovered there have never been identified; some that have are believed to have been the victims of contract hits. In 1989 Terence Gooderham and his girlfriend were found slain by a double-barrelled shotgun after he allegedly creamed off a quarter of a million pounds from the money he was laundering for a well-known crime family. In 1990 Patricia Parsons was shot in the head with a crossbow because it was believed she was about to go public with the black book of clients who had visited her 'massage parlour'. The Kray Twins are also believed to have buried some of their victims there when they ruled London's criminal underworld in the sixties.

The cover provided by the forest has also made it popular as a hiding place. Notorious eighteenth-century highwayman Dick Turpin is said to have had a hideout there. In 1966 ex-soldier Harry Roberts hid there for three months until his capture for the part he played in the murder of three policemen in the so-called Braybrook Street Massacre in Shepherd's Bush. In 2014, a couple out looking for edible mushrooms even stumbled upon a hidden cannabis farm.

Theydon Bois

This unusual village just off J27 (but which we can only access from J26) has kept itself in the dark for centuries, but its refusal to leave the Dark Ages is entirely self-inflicted, the residents voting time and again to have no street lighting on the grounds that it would spoil the look of the village. Its other endearing feature is its Avenue of Trees along Loughton Lane. The oak trees were originally planted in the 1830s and a secondary line is now being grown, set back from the front line, for future-proofing purposes.

The unusual village name arises from the family that held the manor in the twelfth century, referred to variously as Bois or de Bosco in view of their manor's proximity to Epping Forest. In that very British way of adopting foreign words that we lack the basic language skills to pronounce properly (I think the one that annoys me most is Beaulieu in Hampshire), the sound of this one over the years became 'Theyden Boyce' or 'Theyden Boys' (the exact pronunciation seems to vary even amongst residents).

The village's other claim to fame is its annual Donkey Derby. The jockeys are always the village children, while the adults are allowed to place small bets on the outcome of the race. The child that comes last is sacrificed to the forest and the others all get to live for another year.

Lakeside Shopping Centre

J30 and J31 are best known for providing access to Lakeside Shopping Centre, since 1990 the retail pride of the South-east. At least it was until Bluewater came along just over the other side of the Thames in 1999 and left Lakeside looking like it had been there for a while. Make no mistake, though, Lakeside is still going strong after a recent refurbishment, with as many visitors (25 million per annum) and parking spaces (13,000) as its newer rival across the water. There are also a few things Lakeside has that Bluewater doesn't have:

→ A history of starring in its own BBC 'docusoap', first in *Lakesiders* in 1998 and again in *Return to Lakesiders* in 2008.

→ The opportunity to eat succulent Swedish meatballs at the IKEA superstore in the adjacent Lakeside Retail Park. I once went to IKEA while I was in Malmo just to see if the meatballs tasted the same there. They did. Don't forget to have the French fries, cream sauce and lingonberry jam, though.

➔ Lakeside's current owners, intu, are so cool that they don't even need to capitalise their name. It's the twenty-first century way of showing that you are down with the kids. Eat your heart out, 'bluewater'.

➔ A nature reserve out the back, so if you do get fed up with all that shopping, you can just pop over to the Chafford Gorges Nature Reserve to check out the kingfishers, woodpeckers, martins and warblers that are known to frequent the well-stocked, orchid-fringed lakes there.

St Clement's Church

Not far from intu Lakeside (see how cool that is?), down by the river to the east of the QEII Bridge, you can find the fifteenth-century St Clement's Church. When you see it, you will wonder why on earth anyone would want to build a beautiful fifteenth-century church right slap-bang in the middle of all these huge twentieth-century manufacturing plants. The answer, of course, is that the fifteenth century came first, but that only begs the further question as to who allowed such incongruity to happen around this defenceless little church in the twentieth century.

Be that as it may, the church became famous when it starred as the venue for the funeral in the 1994 romantic comedy film *Four Weddings and a Funeral*. Go there to relive the W. H. Auden moment ('Stop all the clocks...') and wonder at the level of acting involved to place yourself in a quaint rural church setting when you are in fact surrounded by heavy industry. If the term 'industrial-strength acting' wasn't coined here, it should have been.

One of the heaviest of these heavy industries is the huge Procter & Gamble factory that has loomed directly above the church since 1940. It's top half resembles a bright-red Lego brick (which you can see clearly from the QEII Bridge), and I have always assumed that they chose this particular design to reflect their red-faced shame at choosing the site in the first place. In 1987, however, they redeemed themselves somewhat by taking responsibility for the renovation and ongoing maintenance of the church after it had fallen into disrepair.

The American business giant is famous the world over for its soaps and detergents, but it has an even better claim to fame than that. In the twentieth century it sponsored a number of American radio and TV programmes, which thereby became known in the States as 'soap operas'. That it should end up with a huge soap-making facility to the east of London was perhaps, therefore, inevitable. If the BBC ever decides to accept sponsored advertising of its programmes, I have an idea for *EastEnders*.

Rainham Marshes RSPB Reserve

One final good reason for exiting at J30 or J31 is the access they both provide to the area that the RSPB has converted from a former Ministry of Defence shooting range to a superb nature reserve on the type of marshland favoured by wading birds in summer and ducks in winter. Cries of 'duck' can still be heard over the marshes, therefore, but they don't mean the same as they meant when the MoD was shooting the place up. Birds of prey are also not unknown to come gunning for the small mammals that frequent the area. All this talk of nature leads us on nicely to the next chapter, which just happens to be called 'The Natural World of the M25'. Continuity is everything in this game.

The Natural World of the M25

↑

> *"He had about the same life expectancy as a three-legged hedgehog on a six-lane motorway."*
>
> Terry Pratchett

Straight from the Essex marshes that we left behind at the end of the previous chapter, we are now going to have a closer look at some of the many species of flora and fauna that inhabit the many different environments of the M25 corridor. You could be forgiven for thinking that the M25 must have destroyed huge swathes of those environments, but Highways England, acting like some kind of modern-day Capability Brown, has in fact planted more broadleaf woodland than any other organisation in the country in recent times, all to protect as far as possible the environment that motorway builders have to cut through. Many of the engineering achievements of the M25 were implemented at least in part to avoid disturbance to the natural world of the waterways and countryside that support so much of the wildlife we hold dear. Not only are the environments and their associated wildlife still there, many of them are wonderfully accessible from the motorway itself. Some wildlife can even be spotted without leaving the motorway at all, as long as you remember to look up sometimes.

BIRDLIFE

Red Kite

Let us start with the obvious. The birds of prey we often see circling above the M25 or perched on top of the road lights are usually going to be red kites or kestrels. Red kites are most commonly seen hovering above the stretch of motorway between J16 and J21 and on the adjoining M40 going north-west from J16, where the sky overhead often resembles a scene from Alfred Hitchcock's *The Birds*. These birds have been hugely successful breeding in this area in recent times, a quite remarkable comeback for a species that was down to one breeding pair in Britain in the 1890s. They are so prolific here because the RSPB and Natural England imported a number of them from Spain between 1989 and 1994 and released them into the nearby Chiltern Hills, part of a wider project to reintroduce the birds to Britain.

They will usually be too high in the sky for us to admire their stunning markings and colours (two-tone rusty red and chestnut, with white patches under their wings and black wingtips), but we can still take in their majestic flight as they glide around with very little effort, their five-fingered wingtips and deeply forked tails outstretched for our viewing pleasure.

They hover above the motorway primarily for carrion in the form of roadkill (whereas kestrels are more interested in the small mammals that are still alive and warm on the verges), so the next time you hit a small mammal or game bird on this stretch of the M25 or nearby M40, console yourself with the fact that you have simply provided a ready meal for a once-endangered species.

The reason that red kites (and other birds of prey) can hover so effortlessly above motorways, incidentally, owes much to the thermals created by the heat our vehicles make, so the part we play in the feeding process is twofold – we make our customers comfortable and then we prepare their meal for them, albeit without giving too much thought to its presentation.

Kestrel

Notwithstanding the number of red kites on the north-western stretch of the motorway, kestrels are what we have been used to seeing hovering above our motorways for years. One breeding pair decided to get even closer to the action when they set up their nest on a mobile concrete production unit being used to widen the motorway through J29 in 2011 – these birds obviously don't know a 'flyover' when they see one. One of the plant supervisors spotted their precarious situation and promptly knocked up a custom-built nest box for them (if you can widen a motorway, you can knock up a nest box). This resulted in the successful hatching of all six eggs. As kestrels remain on the amber list of endangered species, the RSPB have asked more motorways to be widened in the ongoing attempt to grow the number of kestrel around Britain (this might not be true).

Since you ask, the way to tell kestrels apart from red kite is that they are way smaller, with more pointed wings and a long fantail as opposed to a forked tail.

Reservoir Birds

As we saw in the Surrey chapter, just after J13 the motorway takes us between two of the huge reservoirs that provide London with its water supply, Wraysbury Reservoir and the King George VI Reservoir. Given the other four reservoirs that complete the London supply chain, and the five rivers that converge with the Thames in this same area, it is not surprising that the resulting habitat supports many important species of bird, and waterfowl in particular. These include cormorant, tufted duck, goldeneye and great crested grebe, some of which fly in for the winter and fly out again in the spring. You might be lucky enough to see a flock migrating overhead as you drive along, but I don't recommend training your binoculars on them while driving.

Pick 'n' Mix

There are too many country parks and nature reserves to mention within striking distance of the M25, but three of the main ones to visit to see birdlife are Colne Valley Park, Epping Forest and, as we have seen, Rainham Marshes.

Some of the highlights of Colne Valley include all three species of British woodpecker in Old Park Wood in the spring, kingfishers along the River Colne in the summer, goldcrests and treecreepers around Little Britain Lake in the autumn (make sure you have your binoculars at the ready for the goldcrest in particular, as it is Britain's smallest bird), and snipe overwintering in the wet grasslands of Frays Meadow Farm. The alder trees throughout the park play host to small migrants all year round.

The habitat is so diverse in Epping Forest that you are likely to see finches and tits on the woodland floor, chiffchaffs and warblers in the thickets, starlings and skylarks in the grasslands, wildfowl on the lakes and ponds, birds of prey above the tree canopy, and low-flying barn owls at dusk on the edges of the forest where it meets with farmland.

Wherever you decide to go, check the official website of the reserve or park to know what to look out for when and where.

Who Ya Gonna Call? GOOSEBUSTERS!

Shepperton Swan Sanctuary was called out on 20 July 2014 to rescue 25 Canada geese from the carriageway at J11. The four breeding pairs and their 17 young were a bit off-piste, to say the least, because Canada geese do not usually leave their breeding grounds at such an early stage under any circumstances.

Just Swanning About

On 26 July 2014, a disorientated swan had to be removed early in the morning from the fast lane near J13, following which it was taken to the Swan Lifeline charity in Windsor, where it was declared fine. The annual swan upping on the River Thames, when all mute swans are rounded up, marked and rereleased by the Queen's Swan Marker and his Swan Uppers, had just taken place that week, and it had been found that swan numbers were a bit down on previous years (I think I know at least one of the reasons for that).

The Crown has owned all mute swans on the Thames since the fifteenth century, at which time they were considered quite the delicacy, and the Queen today retains the title of Seigneur of the Swans. Capturing one on the M25, outside of the Crown's jurisdiction in such matters, was a clear case of 'swan upmanship' over their boss woman for Highways England employees.

Wild Goose Chase

On 15 October 2014, the M25 anticlockwise carriageway near J9 was closed to allow Wildlife Aid volunteers to run after and rescue a dazed Canada goose wandering along the hard shoulder, having smashed its wing when it crash-landed on the motorway (apparently geese and swans often mistake shiny tarmac for water). It was taken to the veterinary hospital in nearby Leatherhead for X-rays and, with the help of a splint, has since been nursed back to health. It is apparently now living and flying happily around a private lake. It's enough to warm your heart, unless, of course, you were stuck in the ensuing tailback that day, in which case maple-roast parsnips are probably coming to mind. But even then you should probably consider that a large wandering goose on the carriageway might cause drivers to swerve, with potentially horrific consequences.

MAMMALS

Protected Deer Habitats

Deer can be found just off the M25 in a number of important protected habitats. Epping Forest is home to whole herds of fallow deer as well as solitary muntjacs, the oldest deer known to mankind, having been around for up to 35 million years (not the actual ones in Epping Forest, the ones that used to roam the earth a long time ago). These strangely beautiful creatures with Asian ancestry have been on the increase around Britain since a few escaped from country parks like Woburn Abbey about a hundred years ago. Short and stocky, they are about the size of a Labrador, and even have a grunting bark to go with it.

Still in Epping Forest, the deer sanctuary near Theydon Bois has melanistic fallow deer, so called because they are the darkest of the four 'fallow' shades. In fact, their brown is so brown that it is practically black.

Other deer parks to be found within striking distance of the motorway include Knole Park, near Sevenoaks not far from J5, which is home to fallow and sika deer;

Richmond Park, straight up the A3 from J10 (home to red and fallow deer); and Windsor Great Park off J13 (home to red, fallow, roe and muntjac deer).

The measures taken to protect their environments have seen deer numbers double in the last 10–20 years across Britain, where the population is once more what it was at the time of the Norman Conquest.

Oh, Deer!

We will often see road signs warning of deer crossing while driving on the M25. That deer are fairly common within the M25 corridor is not that surprising, because the countryside this distance from London was once totally forested and pretty much commandeered as royal hunting grounds.

The most common time for deer to be spotted, or to cause accidents when they find their way onto the motorway, is at dawn or dusk, particularly during the spring and autumn months. The first half of October is the worst time from a motorist's point of view, for this is the rutting season when the last thing on a deer's mind is road safety.

Living Life on the Verge

The clearance work required to widen the M25 between J5 (Sevenoaks) and J7 (M23) in 2013 revealed an abundance of wildlife on our motorway verges that otherwise goes unnoticed: dormice, great crested newts, bats, grass snakes, slow-worms, common lizards and Roman snails all revealed themselves to the outside world. Bats and dormice are attracted by the food and shelter provided in the long grass, great crested newts breed in the drainage ponds created to take the surface water away from carriageways, and water snakes help themselves to newts and frogs from those same ponds. An enormous amount of time, trouble and expense was put into recreating the disturbed habitat and relocating the small creatures therein, as is the case whenever a motorway is built or widened anywhere in Britain.

Crazy Horses

On the morning of 9 October 2012, a 20-mile (32-km) tailback was caused during the rush hour by the appearance of four loose horses trotting along the anticlockwise carriageway near Potters Bar in Hertfordshire. A similar thing happened as the morning rush hour was getting underway on 7 January 2015, when a loose horse appeared on the anticlockwise carriageway near J28, having escaped from its field near Brentford in Essex. As the horse wandered around looking confused, vehicles with much greater horsepower at their disposal had no choice but to wait until the animal could be rescued.

Illegal Ewe Turn

Thirty sheep invaded the anticlockwise carriageway near J6 in Surrey on 8 January 2014, having escaped from a nearby field. Surrey Police and Highways England officers joined forces to form the necessary posse. They herded the sheep down an embankment to safety but one of them proved more elusive than the rest. It had to be taken into custody in the back of the police van before being returned to the flock by road, though not before it was given a ticket for making an illegal ewe turn.

FLORA

Yellow Delight

One of the great pleasures to be had driving the M25 is to feast our eyes on the striking yellow of rapeseed fields as they flower between mid April and June each year. They provide welcome visual relief for drivers and passengers alike and are as good a reminder as any that we are never far from the calm of rural England wherever we are on the motorway.

Brassica napus, to give it its proper binomial name, is grown for its oil-rich seed and is the third-largest source of vegetable oil in the world (after soybean and palm oil). Rapeseed oil is a versatile product used for human consumption, animal feed, fertiliser, engine lubrication and biodiesel. If you are running a car that is fuelled by biodiesel, you are doubly entitled to enjoy the glory of the flowering rapeseed as you drive along doing your bit for the planet (unless you suffer from hay fever, in which case you're probably not having that much fun driving past rapeseed fields in the first place).

TREES, SHRUBS AND PLANTS

The foliage around the M25 is not just there to hide the motorway from view or to stop us peering into other people's towns and villages. It serves to clean up some of the pollution caused by the hydrocarbons emitted by our vehicles; it creates a natural border between the road and the wildlife that lives in its shadow (that's why there is so little roadkill given the amount of traffic and the abundance of wildlife that co-inhabit the M25 corridor); and, as we have seen, it helps to preserve a suitable habitat for our small mammals and invertebrates. That is why Highways England employs horticulturists and ecologists in addition to the people who toil to keep us moving along the motorway.

Using a variety of trees and shrubs and plants adds interest for the motorist, which matters because soporific boredom is one of the main causes of accidents. But, as we are about to see, sometimes only one tree will do.

Silver Birch

Coming up to J10 clockwise, sand and gravel banks rise up, topped by silver birches, the only trees that can grow on this type of soil. When we see silver birches on their own, there is a good chance we are on one of the very few stretches of the M25 that is not built on either chalk or clay. Geologically speaking, this mixture of sand and gravel is known as Greensand, because the marine sediment it is composed of has greenish grains.

Epping Forest

Of course, if you really want to see a lot of trees close up, you need to pop off at J26. If your arms are long enough, you can hug ancient oak, beech and hornbeam, and a lot more besides. The oldest trees are regularly pollarded (have their top branches cut off) to encourage fresh growth and thereby provide a habitat that supports a wealth of small mammals, birds, bats, insects and fungi.

Ragwort

This bright yellow plant (also known as 'stinking willie') may be pleasing to the eye but is in fact classified as an 'injurious weed' because it can be poisonous to grazing animals. Its seeds can be carried for miles in the wind, making it impossible to eradicate, so Highways England face a constant battle to keep it under control by means of year-round spraying along the M25 corridor.

THE GREATER-SPOTTED, LESSER-WITTED GOLFER

One final species to look out for as we journey round the M25 is the golfer, for this is very much their natural habitat. There are around 200 golf courses within striking distance of the M25 corridor, many of them visible from the motorway itself. You will be able to spot the species by their bright plumage and cries of despair, particularly during the summer months when they herd together in greater numbers than at any other time of the year. Shorn of their winter coats, this is also the time to appreciate the many different shapes and sizes of the species, which is most unusual in the animal kingdom.

The M25 in Popular Culture

> *I have always tried to look at the positive, even when stuck in ten miles of traffic on the M25.*
>
> Alan Pardew, when his job as manager of Newcastle United was under threat

It is hardly surprising that a landmark as infamous as the M25 quickly found its way into popular culture, from music, literature and comedy to TV programmes and films. Here are just a few examples of how the motorway has embedded itself in our psyche:

FREEWAY FOR A DAY

In 1986, Hollywood turned up on an unopened stretch of the M25. They came to film *Superman IV: The Quest for Peace* between J21A and J22, including a shot of Superman (Christopher Reeve) scooping up the car being driven by arch villain Lex Luther (Gene Hackman) and flying off with it. It was probably the one and only time that so many American vehicles, including an iconic yellow school bus, could be seen on the M25, although some eagle-eyed film buffs have pointed out that a few cars with UK licence plates did sneak into view and survive the cutting process.

DRIVING THE M25 FOR FUN

Not long after the motorway opened, BV Leisure brought out 'The M25' board game, which they marketed as 'a bumper to bumper game of bollards, breakdowns and botheration'. During the attempt to complete the circle and thereby win the game, you needed to lip-read what other drivers were trying to say to you and mime what you thought of another player's driving. I'm pretty sure I have seen this game being played for real on the motorway. Why not try it with the drivers around you the next time you are caught in slow-moving traffic? It's bound to be fun.

ORBITAL

Within three years of opening, the M25 had inspired the name of this electronic dance music duo from Sevenoaks in Kent, consisting of brothers Phil and Paul Hartnoll. This was primarily because the motorway was instrumental (pun intended) in getting musicians and partygoers to the rave venues that were springing up around this area of the South-east at the time.

The band went on to enjoy critical and commercial success, an NME music award and a headlining appearance at Glastonbury, the first acid house band to do so. Eat your heart out, Abbey Road!

'THE ROAD TO HELL'

This was the biggest-selling single for English singer-songwriter Chris Rea, penned at J15 of the motorway in 1989 while he sat suffering the frustrations of a rush-hour traffic standstill (as we know from the lyrics, it certainly wasn't a technological breakdown he suffered). The scrap of paper he scribbled the lyrics on that day was sold for charity in 2010.

The song reached number 10 in the British Singles Chart, but climbed higher than that (to number 6) in the Austrian Singles Chart. I don't know why that should have been, given that Vienna's famous *Ringstrasse* is an extremely beautiful and fairly sedate example of a ring road, so much so that Sigmund Freud used to take a daily walk round it to clear his head.

RAVE AROUND THE CLOCK

In the late eighties and early nineties would-be ravers would gather at service stations until word came in that tonight's rave would be held at such and such a venue, whereupon hundreds, sometimes thousands, of ravers could be seen running to their cars to head off in the appointed direction. Cars transporting up to 5,000 ravers fought constantly to outfox the 20 or so police cars used in the authorities' attempts to stop the raves from happening (because, invariably, drugs were involved).

THE CIRCLE OF LIFE

They say you're not really famous until you've been satirised. In 1990, the M25 was the subject of a short musical cartoon about how a man's life went wrong around the motorway. It aired on the award-winning British satirical comedy *Spitting Image*, which was as famous (or as infamous, more like) as it got back then.

BEWARE THE EVIL MOTORWAY

In their 1990 book *Good Omens: The Nice and Accurate Prophecies of Agnes Nutter, Witch*, authors Terry Pratchett and Neil Gaiman make the very useful point that the shape of the M25 forms the dark-magic sign 'Odegra' in the language of the Black Priesthood of Ancient Mu and means 'Hail the Great Beast, Devourer of Worlds'. You have been warned.

SELF-DRIVING THE M25

In 1996 English journalist and political commentator Will Self spent two weeks travelling round the M25 to concoct and present a half-hour documentary for Channel 4 called *J'adore the M25*, a satirical view of the part that motorways like the M25 play in modern society. It was shown once, at one o'clock in the morning, after a programme about log birling. Several years later he wrote a piece lamenting that his effort had been found less interesting by Channel 4 than a bunch of Scottish and Canadian lumberjacks trying to stay on their feet while 'birling' over waterfalls on revolving logs. It may have been some consolation to him that the piece he wrote appeared in the renowned publication *Front Drive: Australia's National Magazine for Citroën Owners and Enthusiasts*, the editors of which clearly recognise good subject matter when they see it, which is more than we can say for the schedulers at Channel 4.

GIMPO

Every year since 1997, on the weekend nearest the vernal equinox in March, a (sort of) performance artist calling himself Gimpo drives round the motorway for 25 hours. He plans to do it every year until 2021 in order to complete 25 x 25-hour orbits of motorway number 25. You at least have to admire the symmetry of that.

M25 RACER

In 2000, the *M25 Racer* computer game jumped on the orbital bandwagon, but apparently wasn't very realistic because cars never got damaged and the police could catch you in a Vauxhall Astra even if you were doing 500 mph (805 km/h) in a DeLorean. A few years later came a version of *TOCA Race Driver*, which had the slightly more realistic option of racing round the M25 in V8 supercars in just 42 minutes at up to 165 mph (266 km/h).

LONDON ORBITAL

English writer and filmmaker Iain Sinclair decided to walk round the M25 just before the dawn of the new millennium and wrote about the experience in his book *London Orbital* (2002). The walk was then loosely recreated for an eponymous documentary road movie that same year, more of a haunting companion to the book than a recreation of it, and a remix of some of that footage was prepared for a one-off performance event at London's Barbican Centre.

Sinclair is influenced by psychogeography, which is the study of the effects of our immediate environment on our emotions and behaviours. It's not difficult, then, to see why he was drawn to the M25.

COCK-A-HOOP

In a 2003 *Top Gear* episode presenter Jeremy Clarkson drove a lap of the M25 in a diesel VW Lupo TDI while another member of the Top Gear team drove a petrol Lupo Sport in convoy, the objective being to monitor the difference in fuel efficiency between the two. The diesel won wheels down and Clarkson spent his savings in a shop in the South Mimms service station. He bought a tacky golden cockerel that was later awarded as 'The Golden Cock' at the end of subsequent *Top Gear* series to the presenter who had made the most embarrassing cock-up during the series.

M25 – TRAVELLING CLOCKWISE

In 2004, taxi driver Roy Phippen decided to put his knowledge of the M25 to good use by writing a book on the subject, partly to satisfy his own questions about his daily surroundings and partly to satisfy the questions posed by his passengers while he ferried them to and from Heathrow and other destinations from his base in Sevenoaks, Kent.

BEYOND BLACK

This 2006 darkly funny and thought-provoking novel by Hilary Mantel is about a medium plying her psychic trade around the M25 corridor. The book contains many a fine description of the motorway and surrounding countryside, albeit in fairly bleak terms, like the 'Heathrow sheep stained by aviation fuel'.

THE M25 AND ALL THAT JAZZ

In 2007, just two weeks short of his 86th birthday, the grand old man of British jazz, trumpet player Humphrey Lyttleton, released his *Cornucopia* album, which included the track 'M25'. He was just as famous for hosting the Radio 4 'antidote to panel games' *I'm Sorry I Haven't A Clue* from its inception in 1972 until his death in 2008.

'OH NO, YOU WON'T!'

While caught up in slow-moving traffic on the M25 in December 2008, former Page Three girl Linda Lusardi dialled 999 to ask if she could have a police escort along the hard shoulder to avoid being late to appear in pantomime as the Wicked Queen in *Snow White* at the Swan Theatre in High Wycombe. Her request was refused and the police made a public example of her to remind people that the 999 number should only be used in real emergencies.

BATMAN STOPS TRAFFIC

In 2009, Fathers for Justice campaigner Geoffrey Hibbert scaled a gantry at J14 and unfurled his banner to make the point that fathers were being unjustly treated by the Family Courts. Police decided to close all lanes on both carriageways because they thought the distraction might cause accidents, resulting in long delays and tailbacks of up to 55 miles (88 km). It was 8 hours before Hibbert eventually came down, and he was subsequently convicted of causing a public nuisance and endangering the lives of others.

ARCTIC CIRCLE

In January 2010, modern-day explorers Rob Lilwall and Alastair Humphreys spent a week walking round the M25 during some of the worst winter weather for 30 years. Their progress clockwise from the Dartford Bridge attracted a huge Twitter following, and locals contacted them to offer food and warmth along the way.

THE ROUNDEST ROUND OF GOLF EVER?

In August 2010, Northern Irishman Trevor Sandford played 31 golf courses, one a day, around the M25 to raise funds for charity. A round of golf was never as round as when it was played on the orbital.

EVERYWHERE AND NOWHERE

In 2011, on the twenty-fifth anniversary of the motorway's opening, the BBC produced a documentary called *The Road to Nowhere*, which examined the impact of the M25 on our environment, economy and living habits. Contributors ranged from those who thought that the M25 had destroyed the countryside and ruined lives to those who appreciated the ability to travel round London quicker than ever before and recognised the huge contribution that the motorway made to the economy of Greater London and beyond. The general conclusion seemed to be that the M25 was indeed the most talked-about road in Britain and that it was either the Road to Nowhere or the Road to Everywhere depending on your point of view.

IN A JAM

Jake Wallis Simons' 2014 novel *Jam* explores what happens when a disparate group of travellers find themselves stuck in an overnight traffic jam on the M25, in an area where there is no mobile phone signal and the emergency roadside phones are out of order. It gets quite tense, but probably not as tense as you'll feel the next time you have to travel the road in the middle of the night after reading the book.

GOING ROUND IN CIRCLES

In November 2014, the Hayward Gallery on London's South Bank commissioned a piece entitled 'I've Been Going Round in Circles Since 1986'. It was a large-scale choreography that involved 15 dancers each walking a section of the M25 so that together they completed the entire orbit. The idea as far as I understand it, which is probably not very far at all, was to encapsulate the parallels between the M25 and the circles that the youth of today find themselves going round in, thereby better understanding the familiar infrastructure of the motorway in relation to human scale and experience. Modern art, eh?

BIG STIG

In January 2015, motorists were surprised to see a giant, white fibreglass sculpture of *Top Gear* mystery test driver The Stig being transported on the back of a lorry along the Surrey stretch of the M25. It was destined for Amsterdam, Berlin and Warsaw to launch a new BBC global channel featuring the *Top Gear* programmes.

COCKNEY REBEL WITH A CAUSE

In February 2015, seventies rock star Steve Harley (without Cockney Rebel) was fined £1,000 and given six penalty points after being filmed speeding at 70 mph (113 km/h) in a temporary 40-mph (64-km/h) zone, even though the road had been all but empty at the time. In order to raise money to pay the fine, an outraged Jeremy Clarkson urged BBC *Top Gear* viewers to download Harley's 1975 number one hit single 'Make Me Smile (Come Up and See Me)'. Within a week over 4,000 downloads at 49p had secured sufficient funds to pay the fine twice over.

DOING THE M25 IN STYLE

Also in February 2015, fun accessories designer Anya Hindmarch put on a show that had the M25 as its theme. It was part of her ongoing experimentation with 'low culture in high fashion'. Her range included triangular handbags with 'Men at Work' signs and the rousing finale was performed by the London Gay Men's Chorus in hi-vis orange and white safety helmets. However much they wanted to be the cowboy, the Red Indian or the traffic cop, they all had to be construction workers that day.

LORD OF THE RING ROAD

In April 2015, a van driver was stopped by police between J5 and J6 when they spotted him watching one of the *Lord of the Rings* films on a DVD player mounted on the dashboard while travelling at 60 mph (97 km/h) in heavy traffic.

Keep Calm and Carry On Driving!

There is understandable concern for the future that the M25 will be unable to cope with the demands put upon it even after it has been stretched as wide as it will go and once smart motorway technology is doing all it can to optimise traffic flows. According to government statistics, there is already just a 54 per cent chance that our journey between J12 and J11 will be 'on time', so either we need to get used to 'being late' or we need to allow twice as long for our journey. If we allow ourselves twice as much time, we will be 'on time' more often than not, at least according to our revised expectations – until the traffic gets even heavier between these two junctions, that is.

Clearly something needs to be done about a rush hour that lasts for three hours in the morning and sometimes even longer at the end of the working day. I assume that more and more people will need to work from home, or work elsewhere in the country, or work different hours. Will some companies eventually be forced into a nocturnal work pattern just so their workers can get to and from their premises? Will more and more deliveries have to be made during the night? Will people start to socialise and visit their families at unusual times?

Perhaps public transport will make more of a comeback once the alternative of people travelling in ones and twos in their vehicles has become completely untenable. The long-term answer will doubtless have to rely on innovative transport mechanisms that nobody really wants to contemplate until there is truly no alternative, like dedicated motorway lanes for public transport vehicles and a ban on single travellers.

Of course, no one can ever legislate for the accidents that are caused by poor driving standards on an almost daily basis, and there is no sign that M25 drivers as a whole are going to wise up any time soon.

In the meantime, we must stay calm and find our own ways of coping with motorway traffic delays as the M25 becomes a twenty-first-century embodiment of the half-empty/half-full glass dilemma. Rage against the machine and it will hurt you. Go with the flow, however slowly, and you may yet enjoy even those days of your life when the M25 is out to get you. If this all sounds a bit too Zen for you, here are my practical tips on how to preserve your sanity on the days you come a bit unstuck driving the orbital.

THINGS TO DO TO STAY CALM ON THE M25

→ Put on some nice, relaxing music (whatever you like, but avoid Chris Rea's 'Road to Hell' at all costs).

→ Look forward to your next holiday (unless you're trying to get to the airport right now to go on your next holiday and you're probably going to miss your plane, in which case move quickly on to the next tip).

→ Smile sympathetically at the people in the cars around you. Remember, you are all in this together and a problem shared is a problem that none of you can do anything about. (Note: if your sympathetic smile looks a bit strained and awkward, like the one the spin doctors taught Gordon Brown to do when he was prime minister, just nod and make eye contact and leave the smile out.)

→ If you are stuck in a monumental jam that's going to make you really late for an important meeting or interview with someone you find intimidating, imagine them naked and they will suddenly seem much less scary. I find this works particularly well when my next meeting is with Kate Winslet.

→ Be grateful that your life is so above average that you can afford to think that being stuck on the M25 for a while is a truly terrible thing. It's not a great thing, I accept that, but many worse things are probably happening at sea. Does this help?

→ Congratulate yourself on allowing so much time for your journey that your current delay is of no real consequence (unless you have not left enough time for your journey, in which case see 'Things to Do to Make Yourself Really Angry on the M25' below).

THINGS TO DO TO MAKE YOURSELF REALLY ANGRY ON THE M25

→ Remember to fill the back of your car with young children (preferably your own) before you set off on your journey.

→ Blame everyone you came into contact with earlier in the day for delaying the start of your journey. Try to include the people you wasted time watching on breakfast television for maximum effect.

→ Make empty promises to your favourite god (or gods) that you will live a better life if he (or she) just gets the traffic flowing again. This will work well until the traffic slows right down again after half a mile, whereupon you might as well resort to blasphemy.

→ Remind yourself that the only reason you're delayed is because you were stupid enough to join the M25 at the same time as tens of thousands of other drivers, and try to imagine how clear it would be if half of you had stayed at home. Was your journey even necessary?

→ Play Chris Rea's 'Road to Hell' over and over again.

THE END OF THE ROAD

I hope you have enjoyed my miscellaneous ramblings as we completed our circuitous, but ultimately circular, tour of Britain's most infamous motorway together. Although it is possible on a clear run with no stops to drive the doughnut in less than two hours, I hope you now realise that it is much more fun to get off from time to time and investigate the many splendid attractions that lie just within or without the M25 corridor. In fact, the next time somebody suggests a 'staycation', or perhaps even a road trip, instead of flying out to Ibiza or Goa, think M25. You know you want to.

About the Author

Ray Hamilton is a freelance writer and editor, whose lifelong passions are languages and travel. He has edited over 70 books on a wide range of subjects, including fiction, politics, history, travel, Radio 4 and classical music. He previously pursued a varied career in government, the highlights of which included multilateral government negotiations in Paris and a number of forays into sub-Saharan Africa.

ALSO BY RAY HAMILTON:

Military Quotations:
Stirring Words of
War and Peace
ISBN: 978-1-84953-327-0
(2012)

Le Tour de France:
The Greatest Race in
Cycling History
ISBN: 978-1-84953-507-6
(2013)

The Joy of Cycling
ISBN: 978-1-84953-457-4
(2013)

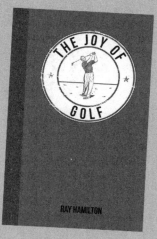

The Joy of Golf
ISBN: 978-1-84953-598-4
(2014)

Trains: A Miscellany
ISBN: 978-1-84953-709-4
(2015)

UNDERGROUND,
OVERGROUND

A LONDON TRANSPORT
MISCELLANY

EMILY KEARNS

UNDERGROUND, OVERGROUND

Emily Kearns

ISBN: 978-1-84953-752-0

Hardback

£9.99

Every year London opens its doors to a staggering 16 million people, all wanting to get to their destination of choice in the shortest time possible. Yet for many of us, the beauty and clockwork of the transport we use, be it taxi, Tube, bus, bike or boat, is a part of the London experience we tend to forget.

From the iconic red buses to the abandoned Tube stations and the engineering achievements to the cultural highlights, this book celebrates everything you've ever wanted to know about getting around in London, and much, much more.

Have you enjoyed this book?
If so, why not write a review on your
favourite website?

If you're interested in finding out more about
our books, find us on Facebook at **Summersdale
Publishers** and follow us on Twitter at **@Summersdale.**

www.summersdale.com